JAZMINE BUNCH

Anesthesia and the Blood of Jesus

From Near Death to New Faith

First published by J Bunch Writes 2024

Names of medical personnel have been shortened for privacy reasons.

First edition

ISBN: 979-8-218-37272-9

Editing by Christie Glascoe
Cover art by Yago Domingues
Proofreading by Alex Robinson
Proofreading by Aaron Bello-Osagie
Proofreading by Maia Morton
Proofreading by Christopher Williams
Proofreading by Gwendolyn Love
Proofreading by Tyree Daye

This book was professionally typeset on Reedsy.
Find out more at reedsy.com

In loving memory of Barbara Collier and Jamaya Roulhac.

And for my brother, Travis Bunch.

"Sit back for a bit and honey, I'll tell you exactly how it feels to be God's favorite…"

TESTIMONY II

Contents

Acknowledgement

A special thanks to people who contributed to my healing and helped make this project possible. To my mom, thank you for everything. To Apostle Jarvis Parker and the entire Kingdom Building family for your effectual, fervent prayers. To my best friends and family, who kept me encouraged and stuck through many interviews while writing. To my new Atlanta friends and family, who've accompanied me in my spiritual walk. To Kennedy, for being there to, quite literally, save my life. To my Alpha-readers and fellow creatives who helped me to polish ABJ. To Khalil Thompson, for all the publishing support. To every single one of you who prayed and donated during my medical emergency, and who are sewing into this God-given assignment by reading right now.

And most importantly, to the God of second chances and rebirths, thank you for another try.

1

Brain on Fire

"And the mind is a terrible thing to waste so the enemy knew to try to attack the exact place where God has this gift of mine..."

Joy and FOMO were competing for first place as my friends' excited screams rang through the phone.

"WE'RE GOING TO THE NATIONAL CHAMPIONSHIP! WE'RE ON OUR WAY TO FRANKLIN STREET!"

Carolina had beat Duke to move on to the final championship game in the 2022 NCAA basketball tournament. Anyone within running distance was on their way to Franklin Street in Chapel Hill, North Carolina, for the traditional rushing of Franklin after a Duke loss. Although I was 377 miles away, my friends Taleah and Gwen called me amid their celebration to make me feel like I was still a part of the action. But as I lay in my bed in the dark–the polar opposite of the party of two on the other side of the phone–I was reminded of something that had nagged me since I'd moved to Atlanta: *You're so far away from home.* To hide my feelings, I bid the gals goodnight, using an early morning as an excuse, and sent them wishes for a safe and fun night in the

Hill.

I swallowed the loneliness that manifested as a lump in my throat before rolling over and looking at memories from Carolina victories and Franklin Street Rushes Past. Even in the good moments, I found myself circling back to that feeling of being alone and so far from home. I'd gone to brunch earlier that afternoon with a homegirl and was oddly still "recovering" from the two cocktails I'd had. I napped it off, charging it to not being properly hydrated. I sank deeper into my warm comforter, happy that my plans to go out that night with a high school friend fell through. Everything seemed fine. It was a normal, uneventful Saturday.

I woke up early the next morning and started my usual Sunday routine. I did my daily prayer and meditation, sat out some shrimp and salmon to defrost for dinner later, and talked to my mom minutes before I turned on the virtual Sunday service livestream as I cleaned my room. It was a typical Sunday morning.

Until it wasn't.

I was on my hands and knees scrubbing my bathtub. The aroma of Clorox disinfectant and citrus Fabuloso wafting in the air, and the sound of worship was the classic combination indicating it was Sunday in a Black household. Suddenly, a painful sensation rushed to my head. I sat up and sat still for a second, initially thinking the products and my position had gotten the best of me. As I sat there, I realized this was no simple lightheaded spell. The pain continued to intensify and heightened into a full-blown headache in under a minute. I stood there gripping my skull and crying out, *"My God, what is happening to me?"*

I'd never felt anything remotely compared to the pain I was feeling at that moment. *Did I inhale too much of the chemicals? Did I mistakenly ingest something? I didn't fall, did I?* Although I constantly played it safe, I didn't rule

2

out the golden question: *Is this COVID?* None of those options made sense in the context of this agonizing pain, but I tried to focus on it in the hope that I could make it go away. As I stood there holding my head, trying to concentrate on my breathing, I thought–this is no ordinary headache.

It feels like my brain is on fire.

Oh man, this is not good.

It had barely been a minute or two, but I started to worry because the pain seemed to get increasingly worse by the second. Like a reflex, I called out to God and rebuked whatever was attacking me. In that same moment, I realized the Sunday service was still playing, and it had gotten to the part of Reverend Raphael Warnock's sermon where he was repeating, "We gon be alright."

We gon' be alright.

There was very little time and room for much of anything, with pain already making itself nice and cozy at the forefront. But this message, seemingly delivered to me at Divine timing, allowed faith and strength to fill the rest of my body to push through whatever was happening. *We gon' be alright.*

Still in immense pain, I knocked on my roommate Kennedy's door to let her know I needed help. Before she could open the door, I crumpled to the floor as the pain started to spread to my ears, neck, and spine. I'm no doctor or medical student, but my math was pretty spot on: That combination and the type of head pain started to add up a little too well.

Oh no. I think something is happening with my brain. Oh no, oh no, oh no.

After a quick exchange of *"what's wrong? I don't know, please help,"* she retreated to the kitchen to grab me water and a warm rag while I struggled to catch my breath. As intense and scary as this was, Kennedy asked me if I wanted her to call an ambulance, and my knee-jerk response was, *"No, I don't know how much that would cost."* In a tag-team between shallow breaths, wrenching pain, and pleading the blood of Jesus, I unsuccessfully tried to take a sip of water. Once I realized the pain radiating down my neck was starting to pair a little too well with the numbness I was feeling in my arms and hands, fear was overruled by fight-or-flight. I told Kennedy I just needed to get up and rest on the couch for a second. I struggled to carry myself across the room, vision blurred, ears ringing, back and neck stiff with each step sending needle-sharp pricks up my spine. I'd gathered up equally as much strength as the hope that our sectional, which usually felt like a cloud, would be the magic elixir to make this pain go away. But the instant I laid down, my body seized up in a way I'd never experienced. I realized it was not going to just go away. I gave in to what was happening and began to cycle through the worst.

Will this be it? Will I really die here in this Atlanta apartment from a freak phenomenon? Will my family make it here? Oh no, my family! Oh God, they just lost my brother, now me?

And just as that sneaky little devil began to creep in and I began to accept defeat, I heard Reverend Warnock's voice again, booming through the room, almost calling me to attention: *We gon' be alright!* It was so strong, yet so comforting. So firm, yet so gentle. So thunderous, yet so quiet. Although the Reverend was at the height of his sermon, and the saints were praising and shouting, with the organ rushing in the background and his voice strong and mighty, the voice of God was layered just beneath it. It was almost like a whisper, speaking directly to me. My family was 512 miles away, but at that moment, my Father's hand was on my shoulder. I knew it was God, and I listened. I refused to accept death, and I began to pray. To plead. To take authority and declare that the devil takes his hands off me. I told Kennedy to take me to the hospital because I refused to lay in the grave the enemy placed for me on that couch.

I took a deep breath, wailed in pain as I pulled my stiff body upright, and walked to the door, praying along the way that I didn't collapse. I prepared for the scariest part: Calling my family to let them know something was wrong. I had to think clearly to decide who I'd call. Once we got in the car, Kennedy located Piedmont Atlanta as the nearest emergency room, and I pulled on all the strength and grit I could to fake it through a phone call with my most level-headed sister, Shadona. I am still waiting for my Emmy to arrive in the mail for the performance I put on:

Deep breath.

"Hey, where are you?" I asked.

"Outside in Pinegate, why?" she countered.

I could hear the chatter of my other family members in the background. "You around, Ma?"

"She's out here, why?"

"So…" *Deep breath.* "Let everybody know I'm headed to the hospital. I don't know what's wrong, but I know something's not right…. BUT I'M OKAY."

"What's wrong with you?"

"I've got a really bad headache. My ears are ringing, my neck is stiff, and my chest is tight. I'm starting to not be able to walk. I don't know what's wrong but something ain't right… BUT I'M OKAY."

"Well, maybe it's just a headache, Jazmine; you know you can over-exaggerate sometimes."

Which was a valid statement, but I realized that maybe it was time to drop the theatrics and be honest with them so there would be a necessary urgency on everyone's part.

The night we got the first call about my brother, Travis, being shot, it was so very random that it couldn't have been serious. So–a thought I never dared to say out loud before–we didn't take it seriously. We all thought it'd be a minor gunshot wound and Travis would act accordingly from now on. A few hours later, we were awakened from our sleep at 4 a.m. to learn that Travis was dead. As much as I held on to my faith that I would make it, I needed them to prepare for that possibility again. While I didn't want to worry them, I wanted them to have the opportunity to do for me what we didn't do for Travis. I needed them to war in prayer.

"Listen. I'm okay, but something is not right. I have never felt a head pain like this before. I'm not being dramatic. This is no ordinary headache."

Dropping the act was easy because the minute I released that stress, the pain intensified, and my body seized up all over again. It was a sobering reminder that life and death lie in the power of the tongue. If I believed and spoke to my sister that I was okay, mentally, I was. But I needed them to prepare for it. Once I spoke uncertainty over myself, the attack found its strength over me again. Kennedy took the phone and explained what was happening to my sister since all I could do was cry out in pain. I heard the tone of my sister's voice change as she relayed the news to everyone outside. They continued to speculate over what it could be: A migraine, the newly inserted IUD birth control, or a sinus infection. I didn't have the strength to explain further, and I felt that as long as they held onto their assumptions, they could hold on to their sanity and I could hold on to my faith. Kennedy wrapped the call with my family, promising to keep them updated.

Out of Downwood, down Howell Mill, and the last I could remember was being stuck for what felt like forever at a red light on Moores Mill Road.

"Kennedy, I feel like I am dying. I need you to put your hazards on and get us there. Fast."

For the rest of the drive, I had no choice but to look to the hills and wait for my Help.

2

We Gon' Be Alright

"Even though sound was fading, and light was blinding, and brain was on fire, I knew–Rev' said it, but God sent it–We was gon' be alright."

Kennedy's gray Honda Civic swung into the emergency unloading zone with an urgency that was not matched by the staff. After running in and alerting the front desk that I was struggling to breathe, see, and walk, a few too many minutes passed before a healthcare worker came out to the car empty-handed, asking me the same information Kennedy had just provided. After I impatiently gave them the rundown of my symptoms, they returned with a wheelchair and instructed me to get in. My spine was sending electric-sharp pain through every limb of my body, so the single step into the wheelchair sent me into a full-on fit. Simply sitting was so uncomfortable at this point that I felt every rock and bump in the gravel as she rolled me toward the emergency room doors, so it especially didn't help that she bumped me into the door. An entirely too-long exchange occurred regarding my insurance before we took our place in the waiting room among the catalog of health-stricken candidates. We'd told them the key things that'd hopefully imply we needed a bit more urgency than what we received when arriving: Trouble breathing, splitting head pain, blinding light, ringing ears, stiffening spine, and what was this new symptom creeping in…nausea? *Uh-oh, definitely not a good sign.*

The moment I felt the pain in my head, I knew it was no regular headache. The fact that it intensified in only a matter of seconds followed by an alarming number of other body functions seemingly shutting down allowed me to quickly deduce that whatever was happening had to be the result of a head injury. I didn't recall falling or hitting my head recently, but a concussion was the most logical thing that I could think of. The nausea rising in my body was the final clue that this mystery emergency might very well be neurological. It was the final flag that prompted the triage nurse to go get me a room and clean it herself.

We were taken to a room with a bed. I was visited by several healthcare workers, to whom I could only round up the strength to beg for the lights to be turned off in between tossing and turning in agony. I was administered a cocktail of nausea, pain and seizure medication via IV injection. I was given a hospital gown to change into, and the lights were graciously flipped back off whenever they left. After a few more visits from unidentified healthcare workers, I was whisked off for a CT scan, a warm rag resting over my face to ease the pain and protect my eyes from the piercing hallway lights. The room was cold and sterile, but thankfully a lot dimmer. I was physically picked up and transferred to the cold, hard table for several attempts to get a clear picture of my brain. I was still riddled with so much pain that it felt impossible to just lie still. After gritting through the pain long enough for them to get a good image, I was transferred back to my bed and wheeled back to my room to wait for the doctor to view the images and hopefully provide some answers. A short time later, a nurse informed me that the doctor looked at my scans and that the neurology team had been called and would be there shortly.

The knot in the pit of my stomach spread like fireworks to my chest.

I'd thought I was experiencing shortness of breath before, but the subtle confirmation that this was a brain-related issue snatched the last bit of my breath away. I started to put the pieces together back at the apartment when my spine began to seize and numb. But faith coupled with denial wouldn't allow me to think the worst. No way something like this could be happening *to me.* I'm too young. I'm healthy. I'd never experienced something like this before. But as I lay in that dark hospital room, wincing and twitching in pain with each breath, I realized the neuro team was coming with news that I probably didn't want to hear. But whether I chose to believe it or not, I decided I'd better brace myself for whatever it was. Across the room, I could hear Kennedy giving updates to my mom on the phone. An Asian man came in, sat by my bed and asked if I could understand him.

"Hey Miss Bunch, my name is Dr. P. We looked at your scans, and you've had a subarachnoid hemorrhage (SAH), which is bleeding on the brain. You had an aneurysm."

Deep breath.

I think at some point, we've all imagined being on the receiving end of a life-changing medical diagnosis. In the movies, the character's heart begins to beat alarmingly loud, the doctor's voice dramatically develops an echo, and the tinnitus, oh man, don't you forget the classic ringing in the ears.

But this was no movie. This was real life. MY real life. And real life just got really scary, really fast. I would've never imagined hearing such news and taking it back like a large pill. I took a deep breath, swallowed, and calmly asked,

"Oh... Where does that come from?"

"Well Miss Bunch, I was going to ask you the same thing. It looks like you're not a trauma patient, you didn't come in from an accident. Did you fall or hit your head?"

"No. I was in the middle of cleaning."

"The only way I can explain it is family genetics or bad luck. Do you have a family history of aneurysms?"

Another no. That statement has been burned in my memory as an automated response.

It's a true testament to the power of God and His authority because I probably should've been terrified. Here I was experiencing this freak phenomenon, and the doctors can't even give me answers. But it was perfect, because if the natural doctors were baffled by the why, then I had no choice but to rely solely on the Supernatural Doctor for the how.

"Okay, doc. Can you call my mom and tell her what you just told me but please, just tell her gently."

My mom is naturally a worrier. After getting a call from a hospital two and a half hours away that her youngest son was dead just two years ago, I truly couldn't imagine how she would react knowing her youngest daughter was lying in a hospital two states away with a life-threatening diagnosis. Though I was physically in a life-or-death situation, I felt like I was going to be okay. All I could think about was my family.

From what I could tell, my mom took the news a lot easier than I thought she would. I heard her over the phone with the doctor, telling him she was eight hours away, but she'd be here as soon as she could, whether by car or plane.

Did she just say something about a flight?

Stephanie Bunch has often stated, *"she ain't getting on nobody's plane, for nothing and nobody.*" But that afternoon, Stephanie Bunch planned to catch a flight to Atlanta if needed. I looked at Kennedy, then back at the doctor and said, "Doc, if my momma comes in on a plane, you can go ahead and prepare a bed for her too."

That warranted a chuckle from him and Kennedy, and I snuck one in myself before the head pain reminded me why we were really here. Dr. P wrapped the call with my mom and stepped out of the room after letting me know that the neurologist and team would provide the next steps.

While waiting, I told Kennedy to call the friends and family she knew to let them know what was happening.

In walked another set of physicians, who introduced themselves as Dr. S the neurosurgeon and his assistant, J.

Dr. S walked me through the first of my options: Emergency surgery. This would take about three to four hours. It'd consist of shaving off a portion of my hair, making an incision on my scalp, and coiling the aneurysm via an artery to close it off and prevent further bleeding. A tube would then be connected to my brain to allow the excess blood and fluid to drain out, and this would warrant a 14-day minimum stay in the Neuro-ICU for monitoring. If this "less invasive" procedure didn't work–because scalping me and going into my arteries messing with my brain juice wasn't invasive at all–then they'd have to do an open-brain surgery that he didn't elaborate on, but mentioned would warrant a longer recovery process. However, he was sure to mention that I should get comfortable, because either way I would be there for, at minimum, the next two weeks. He proceeded to give me all the risks. God knows, there were so many risks.

"...included but were not limited to stroke, paralysis, death, blindness, coma, seizures, nerve injury, vessel injury, groin hematoma, wrist hematoma, leg pain, leg numbness, wrist pain, hand pain, hand numbness, wrist numbness, leg weakness,

hand weakness, radiation exposure, alopecia, renal toxicity, renal failure, allergic reaction to contrast dye, and need for additional treatments..."

He told me I could opt to do neither of these but, of course, he'd recommend taking immediate action. Then he stood there momentarily as if giving me a choice.

Obviously, I want to live. I chose life the moment I began spiritually fighting back against this attack on my physical body. But I had to ask. I needed to know.

"Doc, my mom is on the way here and has an eight-hour drive ahead of her. Is there any chance that I could go in for this surgery and not make it back out?"

With an earnest look I could tell was mastered from years of hard conversations and tough choices; he gave me a nod.

"Nothing is ever certain, there's always risk. But we'll take very good care of you," he said.

With the obvious choice being to proceed with the surgery, Dr. S and J left to prepare the medical masses. We called my mom again to give her an update.

At this point, she was on her way by car with a good chunk of the ride still ahead of her. I gave her the rundown about what they'll be doing and took a moment to be brutally honest.

Deep breath.

"Ma... He said that it's a chance that I could go into the surgery and not make it back out."

"Don't say that. You gon' be alright."

Again. There it was again. That reminder that carried me to Kennedy's room, dragged me to and off the couch, out of the apartment, and here, to this hospital room where I was surrounded by some of the best doctors and medical equipment in Atlanta that insurance could buy.

The voice that gave me a fighting chance. It was God. He was in the pastor, whose sermon reminded me to use my spiritual weapon. He was in my roommate, who's typically not on the same schedule as me and therefore, not usually home when I am. He was in the vehicle when she navigated to the first hospital she could find, which happened to be the correct, parent hospital in a confusing system of hospitals in the area. He was in the triage nurse, who took it upon herself to clean a room for me. He was in the strength of my typically nervous wreck-of-a-mother's voice when she told me I would be okay. He was in the room.

Fear felt useless. It only added fuel to the fire in my brain. There wasn't space for fear as I felt the presence of God in the room with me and in every single healthcare worker who had and would lay hands on me. Although my family was hundreds of miles away (counting down with my mom in transit), I'd never felt more comforted.

I wasn't alone.

A single tear escaped the corner of my eye as I imagined Heaven. Those sterile hospital ceiling tiles became beautiful blue skies and warm clouds. I thought of Travis and wondered if he'd been at peace this way before going, rather than in fear of leaving. I look back on how I thought I'd be so afraid of death when faced with it, and how I'd be emotional and anxious. But in that moment—which I wouldn't realize until a later conversation with my therapist—I surrendered. I'd stopped fighting what was happening to me, and instead of asking God to save me, I prayed that God would have His way. I was the most at peace I'd ever experienced because God was truly in control.

I look back and am amazed at my strength throughout the experience. With the emergency, the diagnosis, the surgery, the needles, the pills. Heck, even the notion of them cutting off my hair would've sent the Jazz of 2019 spiraling. I know now that I was not operating on my own strength. That's the key. That's the difference. When you lean into faith and God more than fear and doubt, you source your strength from a much greater supply than your own and have no choice but to move in that higher power. I truly believe my outcome would have been extremely different had I been afraid, anxious, worried or stressed. The Bible tells us that whatever we ask for in prayer, it's ours. As long as we believe it, we'll receive it. Not only was I bold enough to rely solely on calling on Jesus to save me in the scariest moment of my life, but I was crazy enough to believe it. And it was so.

3

Anesthesia and the Blood of Jesus

"...So, I had no fear because why try to fill the space with doubt when God was already settled into the room?"

I was rolled out of the room and down the halls of Piedmont Atlanta, unsure where I was or where I was going. The concoction of pain meds in my IV were keeping a good portion of the pain at bay, so I had the warm washcloth only covering my forehead rather than my entire face for this ride. I saw blurred white ceiling tiles and flashes of periwinkle medical gloves in my peripheral vision as the surgeon wheeled me through the hallway. As we slowed to enter an elevator, a masked Dr. S looked down at me and gave me a look of reassurance.

"You're in good hands," he said with a smile behind his mask.

I showed some serious restraint, because my first thought was to respond jokingly with my stage name, *"I'm Jazzonfire, I better be!"*

Thankfully, I opted for a more subtle response that triggered a chuckle from the surgeon.

"Good. You're carrying precious cargo, doc," I replied.

For someone being wheeled to emergency brain surgery, I'd bet they thought I was crazy for the level of joy I carried with me through the process. In between life-changing diagnoses and spur-of-the-moment emergency operations, I never lost my joy. I cracked jokes, I laughed when the pain permitted, and I was jubilant as they rolled me down the hallway toward a risky emergency procedure.

If they did think I was crazy, they were right. I had this crazy faith that gave me this crazy assurance that I would be okay. I unofficially made a deal with God the moment I exchanged any ounce of fear for just a mustard seed of faith. I didn't know it then, but my faith was currency paid to the God who gives freely to His children if they just ask and believe. Between needing relief from the inexplicable pain and the little window between diagnoses and surgery, I didn't have time to doubt.

I was rolled into a smaller, chillier, dimly lit room, and was transferred from my bed to a cold, flat operating table. A swarm of medical personnel dressed in teal linen surgical gowns and caps flooded the room. They called their names and respective roles to me followed by the double assurance that I would not remember them when I woke up and they wouldn't take it personally. They moved in swift but fluid motions, wrapping my legs in–what I later learned were–compression sleeves to prevent blood clotting, attaching EKG patches to my chest to monitor my heart, slipping a blood pressure cuff on my arm, and connecting my IV line to begin administering anesthesia. The table buzzed under me from a nearby machine, so had their surgery scrubs been yellow, I might've honestly hallucinated being surrounded by a colony of busy bees.

I was offered warm blankets and assured they'd take good care of me. But at this point, my hope was beyond the people who were physically in the room. Although I felt oddly comfortable on that two by seven-foot table wrapped in warm blankets and connected to every medical machine possible, my need to speak to God went beyond a hushed whisper or inner dialogue. Looking back, I realize it could've been pulling on supernatural strength for someone else in that room, but I felt the need to pray out loud.

"Hey, if you hear me talking or see me gesture, I don't need anything from you all. I just need to pray out loud right quick, if that's okay," I said.

And as they continued prepping to put me under, I began to outwardly converse with God in the most natural, casual way. I felt like I was talking to a friend. A friend that I'd known for years, whom I trusted with my life. A friend that was in the room.

"God... I don't know what part of the plan this is, or what chapter this is going to be, but I just know when I come out on the other side, it's going to be one heck of a story..."

The anesthetic began to kick in as I continued this outward expression of faith, pulling on words I didn't know I had and some I can't recall.

"You're in the room. I feel you. So, I pray that you work through every nurse, assistant and surgeon in this room..."

"We're going to put this mask on you, and we just need you to take deep breaths and just relax, okay?" one of the medical personnel softly interjected.

Deep breaths.

"...Work through the hands of the surgeon. Allow him to recall any and all knowledge he'll need to successfully complete the surgery..."

And the rest of my prayer trailed away into anesthetic murmurs as my body fell into a sedative sleep.

* * *

The white blur of the hospital ceiling filled my vision again as I slowly opened my eyes and began to register where I was and what was happening.

"Hey, you're awake," Dr. S said.

Dr. S. The neurosurgeon. Hospital. I'm in the hospital. I'm awake. I'm alive. I made it. Thank you, God. I made it.

"I made it. Thank you, God. I made it." I said aloud.

A joy I pray I'll continue to experience a lifetime of flooded over me. My hands instantly went into the air after confusion took its course and quickly moved out of the way for reverence. Tears rolled down my face and through raspy whispers, I gave God His due praise.

"Thank you, Jesus. Thank you, thank you, thank you."

Dr. S looked down at me again, with a grin I could almost feel through the mask.

"Something told me you'd say that," he said.

I'm sure it was a sight to see. A bed rolling down the hallway with a singular arm floating in the air from a recently sedated patient. I have no memory of ever being put under general anesthetic before, so this experience of waking up felt like more than a natural experience. As I laid there, minutes removed from a sedative state, having a breathing tube down my throat, and a dice-roll away from any of those many risk factors, I felt this sense of being refreshed. Revitalized. Almost new. I could only compare it to the feeling of emerging from the water after a baptism.

So, there I was, rolling through the hallways of Piedmont Atlanta's neuro-intensive care unit where I'd be recovering for the next 14 days: Hands in the air, flooded with emotion that God brought me out. And as if I'd been baptized in anesthesia and the blood of Jesus, it felt like I'd been reborn.

* * *

Kennedy walked into the room with my overnighter on her arms and a comforting smile on her face. We'd just met in 2021 when I moved into the apartment with her, so it especially touched my heart that she stayed.

"I brought you some stuff from home," she said.

"Thank you."

I noticed she was trying to examine me without letting what she saw show on her face. "Alright, how bad is it?" I asked.

"It's not that bad…" she said hesitantly. "It's a lot…"

I'm not sure I was the most convinced. "You have my phone, right? Take a picture."

I opted for a tongue-out pose first, because… you know… why not? Then I proceeded to give serious kiss-face realness as she giggled and snapped, hovering over me for a close-up of the surgery area.

"Let me see," I said.

"You sure you want to?"

I'd been pretty strong all day, but from the uncertainty in her voice I could assume it was a sight that maybe I didn't want to see fresh out of surgery.

"Yeah, you're right. Maybe I won't," I said as we both laughed.

She sat across the room, and we continued talking as time passed. She did most of the talking, as my throat was still sore from intubation. She relayed the post-surgery updates from the doctors and gave me an update on all the worried loved ones she'd been playing secretary to on my phone as she scrolled through messages.

"Girl, it's the third of the month. We gotta pay rent," she said.

As if I didn't just survive a traumatic brain injury, a wave of worry rushed over me. We hadn't paid April's rent yet. After a brief exchange of whether rent was late on the third or the fourth, I guided her through my bank log-in so she could Zelle herself my half and get it paid.

What a testimony. Just a handful of hours ago, I was writhing in extreme pain as the doctors read an overwhelming list of what-ifs like stroke, paralysis, blood clotting, loss of speech. But here I was no more than 15 minutes post-intubation and anesthesia, paying rent and exchanging pleasantries. What a God.

A nurse came into the room for what looked to be a mindless check-in and instantly did a double take.

"Miss Bunch, you're awake? Oh, my goodness, you're wide awake. Let me go get the doctor."

Her confusion showed me that I shouldn't have been as lively as I was.

The surgeon came in and gave us the rundown of my procedure, mostly directed to Kennedy since I was still coming off the anesthesia. The procedure was a success with no complications. They made a linear incision across my scalp that led to a small, circular hole in my skull using a handheld drill. They implanted coils into the aneurysm to close off and protect the area from further bleeding. An external ventricular drain (EVD)—or as I called it, the brain drain tube—was inserted into the hole in my skull to drain cerebrospinal fluid from the aneurysm site. The linear incision was then closed and the EVD was stapled to my head. It was critical that I lay flat in bed for at least 12 hours. I was informed that the incision site would be sore and that headaches were common, but the goal of the procedure was to relieve me of the intense pressure I was initially experiencing. Job well done, docs.

The splitting headaches were gone. All that was left was general soreness at the incision site, a subtle but manageable headache, and the drowsiness from the anesthesia.

I was reminded that I'd be in the neuro-ICU for the next 14 days minimum for monitoring, because the procedure made me a high-risk candidate for strokes, blood-clotting and vasospasms. Initially, I'd be on a strict cycle of medication for pain management and preventative care. I was restricted to bed rest, bedside baths only, and opted for the PureWick external catheter over a bedpan. The PureWick was a urine collection system that allowed me to use the bathroom without getting out of bed. Finally, I received the strict instructions that I had to call a nurse if I needed to be adjusted, as my brain needed to always be level with the device attached to my EVD that was constantly monitoring brain pressure and ensuring the fluid was draining properly.

"It's going to be a long road to recovery," one of the nurses told me.

I was always very present in the hospital, and surprisingly calm and collected throughout. I didn't know what the future held, the timeline for my recovery or if I'd ever physically be the same. But I woke up feeling normal—minus the excruciating head pain—as before I went into surgery. Honestly, I can't explain why I felt so detached from the severity of what happened. I felt the soreness in my head from the incision. My throat was scratchy from the endotracheal tube, and I was a little groggy from anesthesia, but I felt like I'd simply taken a good nap. I woke up with my memory, all my senses, my physical abilities, and even my witty sense of humor that kept my spirits up post-op. I woke up still feeling very much like me. Though that was a major blessing, considering the exhaustive list of side effects and risk factors going into the surgery, this miraculous condition immediately following helped me to forget just how severe my condition was and just how different everything could be. I don't take lightly the fact that I made it out alive from the surgery or the rupture, but I think the blessing of waking up feeling just like normal—refreshed even—grounded me in faith rather than fear.

Dr. S stood at the foot of my bed after taking me through a minimal postoperative physical while I lay flat. He shined a flashlight, gave some commands, and checked my pupils. When everything checked out, he took a deep breath as he put away his flashlight.

"You are a walking miracle," he said.

The nurse in the room cosigned how the unit was full of stroke and neurological-related patients, and agreed they had never seen anyone, especially someone so young, come back from an aneurysm the way I did.

After drifting off to and through another post-anesthesia nap, I awakened to nurses shuffling around my bed doing their respective tasks. One was adjusting my sheets, another checking my blood sugar, while the other was preparing my next round of medications at the computer. I was exchanging pleasantries with the nurse taking my blood sugar when the room door flung open. My momma had eight hours of wondering, worrying and praying and was now ready to lay hands. She was every bit of five feet tall, with her signature slicked-back ponytail and chocolate brown skin adorned with the dermal evidence of being a mother. Her face was masked, but I could make out both worry and relief in her eyes as she finally laid eyes on her youngest daughter after a day of only hearing worried sentiments and grim diagnoses via phone. She came in the room like a woman on a mission, every step accompanied by a sling of Holy Oil and a whispered plea of the Blood of Jesus. When she got to my bed, she began anointing every part of my body while praying, lathering olive oil in any place she could reach that wasn't being occupied by a nurse.

"I'm sorry if I'm in your way," she said to the nurse at the head of my bed.

"Oh, don't be sorry, I'm a deaconess, so I completely understand. Let me get out of *your* way," the nurse replied.

As my momma and Deaconess Nurse swapped places, she carefully cradled my cranium in her olive oil drenched hands. She brought her face close to mine, offering hushed praises of gratitude to God. I closed my eyes and inhaled as the poignant scent of olive oil and hand sanitizer combined became an aroma I would've given anything to bottle up and keep bedside. I'd been holding it together, mostly because I'd been pulling on supernatural strength, but also because I had no other choice. But my momma was here, right here, physically and spiritually lifting me up so I didn't have to carry this heaviness alone. According to her, she stayed there with me no more than 30 minutes since I was still drowsy from the anesthesia. She'd arrived well after visiting hours, but they made the exception to let her in. The nurse gave her the rundown of my condition, told her everything looked good, and she returned to my apartment a lot lighter after an excruciatingly long and heavy day. I soon after dozed off into another bout of post-sedation sleep.

As the youngest, I'd always been a momma's girl. But that moment would be the first of many to truly remind me that you are never too old to need your momma.

4

Surrender

"..Because it's just something about knowing that I am walking in so much Grace, being physically reminded that I am moving in so much power..."

If I'm being completely honest, the first few days in the hospital were a blur. I remember bits and pieces in between Percocet cocktails and piercing head pain so intense that I couldn't open my eyes. But I remember waking up the first morning of my stay, cautiously opening my eyes and allowing the light peeking through the closed shutters in the room to seep into my vision. With how dim they'd kept the room pre- and post-operation the evening before, I'd honestly thought I'd died and gone to Heaven. And the angel standing over me humming—with her brown skin and matching curls—didn't make it any harder to believe.

"Well good morning," she began. "I'm Nurse P and I'll be your nurse for the day. Can I get you anything?"

Her voice was warm. Comforting. Familial. If I hadn't died and gone to

Heaven, waking up to a black woman with a fresh twist-out in this hospital was going to be the closest I'd get.

"Yes, actually," I said. "My hair is in two braids and they're really uncomfortable, probably causing my headache. They told me last night they couldn't touch my hair, but could you please take them out for me?"

Nurse P's face twisted in disbelief under her mask. I later registered that the look on her face was in response to my very first instance of medical racism. I didn't think much of it. After all, these surgeons did just technically save my life. But on the flip side, you mean to tell me you could do all of that, but you can't unbraid two simple pigtails?

None of that mattered as she gently massaged my scalp after undoing the braids. Relief flooded over me: First, through my neck because those wig braids were most definitely half the cause of my headache. But relief found its way creeping through my entire body because once again, God had physically manifested to remind me that I would be okay—and well taken care of at that. Nurse P and I continued to chop it up as she informed me of my morning routine for the next two weeks. I'd be provided with my daily cocktail of pills consisting of oxycodone and Tylenol for pain, Keppra for seizures and Nimodipine for vasospasms. Someone would check my IV line to see if they could get a clean draw for blood work. I'd have my blood pressure taken and my blood sugar read. I'd be given a PureWick for the day since I was restricted to bed rest and I'm not a bed-pan gal. I was also informed that I couldn't move without a nurse knowing—literally–because the tube they had attached by seven staples to my head was a drain from my brain. This allowed the excess blood and fluid, or what I called "brain juice," to flow from the area where the aneurysm had ruptured.

In addition to the tea on what the road ahead looked like, she also dished the tea on the hospital food in a black container on the tray next to my bed.

"Go ahead and prepare yourself, girl. I don't have high hopes for the tea," she said.

And she was right. I took a sip as she salted the food we both knew was a lost cause. Bacon, eggs and breakfast potatoes. How hard could they butcher that? After a single bite of each thing, I had a handful of ways in mind. Without much of an appetite anyway, we decided we'd wait for my mom to bring me some food when I felt up to eating. I'd given up control the night prior, completely surrendering to God's Will for my life. But now I was being forced to surrender again. This time, 14 days of privacy and control. Echoing the sentiments of the nurses from the night before, it would be a long road to recovery.

Another statement one of my many nurses made was that the hospital was no place for rest. A part of me thought it was a joke, and the other part was so high off pain meds I thought maybe my brain had just ingested the words incorrectly. But she was not kidding. I was on a two-hour increment for the medicine given to me to prevent vasospasms and strokes, and with the type of aneurysm that I had, I was very susceptible to both stroke and seizures. Additionally, my blood pressure required constant monitoring because sodium levels directly correlate to pressure on the brain. I was also constantly being visited by the neuro-physicians doing their routine checks to ensure I wasn't going blind, experiencing paralysis, and that this ol' brain of mine was still sending all the right signals to all the right places. Of course, I had to ensure them that I love a challenge, and by day four, I practically had the routine memorized as the doctor walked in the door:

"Heyyy doc!" I said cheerfully with my arms raised, ready for my daily test.

Arms up. Grab my fingers. Squeeze. Push me away. Pull me to you. Good. Left leg. Right leg. Hold them both up. Hold it, hold it. Good. Wiggle your toes. Do you feel this? Where am I touching you? Bright light coming, look at me. Good. How many fingers am I holding up? Good. Everything looks good.

Everything looks good.

It almost felt like a given. I was so blessed to have gone through what I did and still be in physically good condition. But being in infectiously good spirits regardless of my situation, is a joy I can truly only attribute to God. How good it felt knowing God had His eyes on me.

I was one of God's favorites, no doubt. But I think it's safe to say that I became the favorite of every nurse and doctor caring for me in that neuro-ICU unit too.

* * *

I'd learn as the weeks passed, each day would be different, some much harder than others. My first morning was great. I woke up easily in very little pain and feeling surprisingly energized after getting bursts of sleep between medicine administration and monitoring. Others, like day two, would start very rough. Pain would flood my head the moment I opened my eyes, leading to mornings spent in total darkness hiding from the sunrise that threatened to leak through the rolling, blackout shades.

After locating my phone and responding to a 7 a.m. "you up?" text from my mom, we started what became our neuro-ICU routine: She'd shoot me a text in the morning checking in before heading to the hospital as early as visiting hours allowed. She sat bedside, eyes full of concern. She kept me company throughout the day, offering massages to help ease my discomfort and playing secretary to the influx of concerned calls and texts from family and friends. She'd pray with me as I lay awake and pray over me through every nap, only leaving at the last minute possible when visiting hours were over at night. She strolled in every morning: Bible in one hand, coffee in the other, offering every bit of strength I knew she could only be sourcing from

God to keep me covered and lifted as we fought through recovery together.

Morning one, I got her flood of texts after confirming I was up for the morning.

"You up?"

"Ok."

"We coming."

"You okay?"

Much of day one and two are a blur, a series of moments between long naps and heavy medication, but according to texts, she arrived an hour later. She entered the room much calmer this go-round, still murmuring prayers and slinging holy oil, touching every body part that wasn't occupied by wires, machinery or an IV line.

"God is so good," she whispered. "The doctors said everything is looking good."

"Ma, can you get my phone and play that song, 'Jesus is my doctor?'" I asked. "I want to hear that."

I was back in eyes-shut, hot-rag level pain, so staring at a phone screen was unbearable for most of the first couple of days.

"Can you hold my hand?" I asked.

She found her way to YouTube and Georgia Mass Choir's, "Come On in the Room." I don't quite remember when or where I'd heard this song, but it was tugging on my spirit to hear the words and make the declaration alongside the singers. We sat there in that dark hospital room, me in the bed, eyes shut and her standing over me holding my hand, singing that throwback together.

"Jesus is my doctor, and he writes out all my 'scriptions..." we sang, "...Come on in the room."

That simple moment felt so powerful. If you've ever heard the song, it's just an organ, a man telling the story, a choir and a live audience cheering in the background. But as simple as it felt externally singing this song, I knew it was a reason God placed the desire on my heart to want to hear it in the first place.

It was a prayer. A promise. An invocation. An unintentional moment that became an intentional declaration that no matter how much medical equipment or personnel surrounded me, I would believe in The Ultimate Doctor. The True Healer. The Miracle Worker. The Man I'd come to know so very personally as Jehovah Rapha. So that moment was reassurance of just that. The song continued to play, and I laid and listened, soaking in the presence of God I felt settling in as we invited Him into this moment, this hospital room and this fight.

"...Come on in the room."

* * *

A daily transcranial doppler (TCD) study was introduced to my daily regimen on day three. It's easiest explained as an ultrasound for the brain. Each morning, a medical technologist would roll the machine into my room, usually after I had eaten and taken some pain medicine, and used the device to gather information about the blood flow to and within my brain. A cool, sterile gel was applied to different areas of my head then the part of the device collecting information, was held in place at those points. The procedure was noninvasive and done with the lights off. I had to be still and quiet, while the device was placed on the back of my neck, my forehead, my temples, and behind my ears at different pressures to get the best reading. Depending on the technologist, I had the option to lay completely flat in my bed with my head propped up by a pillow, or to be sat up during the procedure. The soft murmur of the machine and sonorous swooshing of blood flowing in my brain that amplified through the receiver mimicked white noise and ocean sounds, so depending on the day, this was either really relaxing or extremely uncomfortable.

* * *

"Jazmine, you've got to take the medicine," my mom pleaded.

I wasn't the biggest fan of oxycodone for several reasons. Opioid addiction was a valid concern. But the medicine made me feel woozy and weak, almost like a phantom of myself. I couldn't deny that it helped alleviate the headaches, but everything felt so slow and heavy when I took them. It just felt like it was already so much being taken from me, I needed to feel some sense of self, some sense of normalcy. I unintentionally accepted the headaches if the days didn't feel so long, and the drugs didn't make me feel so little like myself. It was depressing enough that I was confined to the four walls of ICU-5A, but to be drugged within them all day was where I drew the line.

"Ma, I don't want to. They make me feel high," I countered.

The nurses recognized the control freak in me and took the liberty of writing my rotating schedule for pain meds on the board. Tylenol every four hours. Naproxen every six hours. Oxy only every 12 hours, so we'd save that for the morning when the pain was seemingly the worst. But who wants to wake up just to sleep all day? Whenever I took them, I'd be alert and present one second and knocked-out cold, mouth wide open in the next. I'd opt for Tylenol and Naproxen instead, and just pay the cost of being wide awake and aware.

"She doesn't want to take her medicine, but she needs to because she's in pain. I know it," my mom said on the phone.

I don't know who in the world was on the other end of the call, but I didn't have the energy to fight her on it. I was fighting hard enough to stay awake and present, which caused half the hurting. Had I exerted as much energy into resting and letting God fight for me and my body fight for itself, I'm sure the first few days would've been much less painful.

My surrender came in waves. I'd realized, sure I surrendered to God before the operation, but I didn't realize I had to keep surrendering. Keep trusting. Keep my faith up and in Him. Why try to fight this pain on my own when I serve a God who heals all? A God who healed me?

Whenever a challenge presented itself, He always proved Himself to be mightier. I'd just recently learned how to swallow pills during my sophomore year of college, so I worried that the oversized Nimodipine pills would be a problem for me. I'm also not a fan of needles; apparently, neither were my small veins. So, the incorporation of a daily anti-blood clotting shot directly in my stomach in addition to a round-the-clock IV catheter proved to be a persistent problem.

My phrase for the duration of my stay became 'there are just much bigger fish to fry,' and to top it off, God was bigger than every single one of them. *I can do all things through Christ who strengthens me,* Philippians 4:13, rang through my mind as I realized that if I'd been spiritually empowered to make it through a brain bleed and non-invasive surgery, surely I can bear the brunt of a few big pills and small pokes. And it was so.

Except for a few mind-over-matter moments where those things would just not go down, it was unbelievable how easy I tossed those 30 mg pills back each round. When it came to those pesky needles, the technique was in the breathing. In addition to calming my nerves, it also made it easier for them to find the veins for a proper blood draw. The big things felt easy. Those big things were simply no match for my big God.

In the beginning, I was in so much pain that I was happy to be surrounded by people that could monitor it and things that could alarm them to do so. But I won't deny the small fear in me that wondered if this would be my life now: Being overwhelmed with pain and feeling reliant on doctors and medicine. This, coupled with one of those bad days the nurse spoke of in the latter half of week one sent my spirits pummeling.

It started as a hard morning, waking up immediately in pain and having had little sleep. It was sure to be a lights-off, shades-closed kind of day. Although I'd had my morning pain medicine, the TCD did not tread the area of relaxing this morning and only agitated my headache even more. I didn't know if it was extra sensitive because I was already in pain, or if the tech today was being far from gentle, but it was becoming increasingly unbearable.

I could feel the impatience radiating from the "almost done," she shot me as I slightly wriggled and writhed.

Whew, not soon enough.

"You want it hot or cold?" my momma asked as the tech rolled the machine out of the room.

"Hot, please," I answered.

Running the washcloths under the running water and pressing it over my forehead would provide moments of relief when the headaches were bad. There were hot compresses for the pressure headaches where it hurt to hold open my eyes, and cold compresses for when my head throbbed, and it felt like my brain was having a thrasher. But today, my hot rag was no help.

"Ma, I'm tired."

"Take a nap, you need some rest."

"No, like, I'm tired...of this."

I let my guard down for the first time since I was rolled through those doors a few days ago. My spirits fell and I gave into fear. I entertained the thought of dying, and whether that would've been easier than this: The pain. The medicine. The lack of privacy and the inability to do for myself. The headaches, my God, the headaches.

"The doctors said you're gonna have headaches and it's not gonna be easy. It's a long road ahead of you so you just gotta take it one day at a time," she said before sneaking in, "and you've got to take that medicine, Jazmine."

She was strong, but I felt the weight of worry she was hiding behind prayer. I saw the concerned glances she tried to conceal when I noticed. I felt the heaviness she was holding each day seeing me in all conditions of recovery. And as much as she was there to care for me, I was also trying to care for her. As odd as it sounds, I tried not to worry her too much, so I stayed optimistic and tried to smile through the pain. But that day, I was in so much pain that I didn't care to fake it. I wanted it to end.

I don't think I can do this. I don't want to do this anymore.

I didn't say it out loud, but she felt it. She knew what I was implying. Silence fell over the room, and I eventually dozed off into a nap. When I woke up, she was perched at her post, Bible open, silently reading and praying.

"Do you feel better?" she asked.

"Yeah, a little bit."

"I called the 700 Club and requested prayer for you," she said. "You want to call Apostle Jarvis?"

Apostle Jarvis was my hometown church's pastor. He and the entire Kingdom Building family were faithfully praying for me all the way from Ahoskie, North Carolina. We even caught the entire church on a FaceTime call at the end of a Tuesday night prayer service early in my hospital stay.

After a brief, generic check-in, his prayer began to fill the room from the speaker phone. Every word he spoke over me was exactly what I needed without telling him what I felt. It was a spiritual weapon against every mental attack that was planted in my mind from the moment I woke up this morning. I thought about how I could die. I thought it'd be easier to just die. Although my mom was there, I felt so alone. I felt the weight of recovery becoming heavier and heavier. But he reminded me that my fight was much bigger than physical. He reminded me that I wasn't fighting alone. He reminded me that I am not dead, and I didn't die for a reason.

"God said you shall live and not die…" he declared.

I was already open to receiving a word from God, because all day the throbbing in my head and the thoughts of the enemy just seemed to be so much louder. But that declaration was my recharge and reminder amid feelings I dared not voice out loud. If I was supposed to die, I would've been dead. I would've gone out to the club as planned the night before, came home drunk and possibly died in my sleep. I would've woken up that morning and possibly gone into a coma had Kennedy not been home, like usual, to take me to the hospital. I would've gone to a different hospital that didn't have a neuro team that came onsite for emergency patients. God is so very intentional. He orchestrated everything the way He did until this very moment to keep me here. God saw fit to keep me alive and He wasn't just going to leave now.

My problem was that I stopped surrendering. I was so focused on being the miracle that I no longer relied on the Miracle-worker. I didn't get this far just to get this far, and I certainly didn't get this far alone. Tears streamed down my face as every word he spoke over me canceled every lie of the enemy and confirmed every promise of God.

I could do this. I can do this. I am going to get through this. We are going to get through this.

"…in Jesus's name we pray…" Pastor Jarvis finished as we simultaneously sealed his declarations.

"Amen."

"We're keeping you covered in prayer, daughter," he said. "You're going to get through this."

The Word tells us, specifically in the King James Version of James verse five, that the "effectual, fervent prayers of the righteous availeth much." Having the man of God speak truth into and over me after such a hard day was just what I needed to keep fighting. I knew the heaviness I felt wasn't just physical, but I also knew I wasn't fighting alone. I knew I had a family of believers pulling on Heaven for me. We told the Apostle goodnight, and I left that call feeling lighter. Freer. Braver. Stronger. Not because I felt like I could do it, but because I knew that God could.

I knew I'd have to be strong and fight through recovery, but a part of that strength was understanding where it wasn't my fight. Thankfully God's strength is made perfect in our weakness, so what use was it to deny God a chance to show just how strong He is? I let go and decided to take the oxycodone when I needed it to get ahead of the pain. I'd ride the wave of mouth-agape naps from my recliner chair, and heavy midday snooze sessions that gave my brain, body and mom a well-needed break.

On day four, a new masked face walked through the doors with a new addition to the routine: Getting out of bed!

I was restricted to bed rest with very strict instructions to call a nurse any time I needed to adjust my position. The drain's position had to be adjusted whenever we modified the bed's position. It had to remain level with my ear so they could closely monitor my intracranial pressure (ICP) level.

It was a good day. The pain was at bay, and I had a good energy level, so I was more than ready to finally get out of bed. She explained how physical therapy would work, especially with all the cords and machinery I was attached to. When I needed to be mobile, I was disconnected from the large EKG in the room and reconnected to the smaller, mobile monitor. The device on my finger continuously monitoring my oxygen levels was unplugged from the connector running to the monitor, with the short end of the cord looped around my wrist. My IV line was closed and capped, and my EVD and brain juice bag were transferred to my mobile cart. We'd try standing first, and if I felt sturdy enough, we'd practice taking a few steps to the bedside chair.

Aced it.

From there we practiced sitting, to see if I could sit up comfortably, and then slowly stand again. While it felt so good to be temporarily back on my feet, the act took so much energy. While I was sitting, she explained how well I was doing and said that we could go for a walk around the unit if I was up to it.

After an enthusiastic 'yes' from me and protests of *"take it easy, Jazmine"* from my mom, she went to find a mask for me and an additional hospital gown to properly cover my exposed backside.

Standing from the chair, I stretched my legs and back to shake off the stiffness. Contrary to the name, bed rest is dreadful on the body. My legs would get numb and feel like dead weight at times. I was starting to experience back and tailbone pain from laying or sitting all day, and my wrists were feeling the effects of constantly lifting and shifting my body weight in bed since I wasn't using my lower body.

In addition to getting my lower half used to standing and walking again, my brain also needed to catch up. Standing reminded me of that feeling when you hang upside down for too long and the blood rushes to your head, but just not as intensely. The discomfort wasn't to the point where I was in pain. I figured it was normal since I hadn't stood in four days, so I took a few deep breaths, pushed through the soreness and told the nurse I was ready to go.

We slowly walked toward the hallway, each step accompanied by a prayer that the fuzzy, yellow non-slip socks would do their job. My mom wasn't far behind, camera in hand and eyes full of caution.

For the first time, I could see where I was and what was just a few feet away from me outside the door. The nurse's front desk station was directly adjacent to my room, with a large plastic shield surrounding the desk. A bulletin board was decorated with an arts and craft garden beneath "Neuro-ICU" in cutout pastel letters. The walkway split in three, with the hallway stretching left and right with a shorter hallway straight ahead, running adjacent to the help desk leading to another side of patient rooms.

"Whatttt, there's 'outside' my room?" I said sarcastically.

After a chuckle from the nurse, she asked if I'd like to play some music and what kind, to which I responded 'gospel' without hesitation.

We paused outside the door while she searched for a song appropriate for the walk, something upbeat and victorious. After failing to properly recall the lyrics to the chorus of Kirk Franklin's "F.A.V.O.R," my day nurse, the second black nurse I'd had, came to the rescue with an entire playlist.

"Here you go, just take my phone," Nurse K said as she queued up some Kirk.

After properly selecting the vibes, we strolled down the neuro-ICU unit. I picked up the pace but was still cautious because it felt almost foreign to do an act I'd once done so freely. My body was sore from lying down for the past 96 hours that it felt so heavy just carrying myself. In addition to physically maintaining my balance, it felt like I was walking a tightrope; a delicate balancing act of walking in my recovering physical freedom and trying not to overdo it.

"You can sit for a minute if you need to," the PT said as we approached a bench.

"I'm okay, it's just a little hot with the mask."

I'd also not worn a mask since the surgery, so toss that into the mix of first-time-since factors and we've got quite the feat. After my small break, we kept moving down the hallway and I felt like I stepped into a medical museum. The dual monitor computer stations lined the hallways with graphs and additional machinery for patient rooms waiting to be tapped in. We even passed the magic blanket warming machine that produced the endless supply of heated blankets.

As I stared in heartache for the patients whose rooms we passed by, the staff in passing would do a double take or give me a small handclap as I walked by.

"Oh, they're going to stare at you because this isn't normal," she said as I shot her a confused glance, "Patients don't just get up and walk around the neuro-ICU."

I gathered that as I peeked in patient rooms during our stroll. I caught a glimpse of the people laying in their rooms so lifelessly and alone–with fully shaved heads and tethered to breathing machines–as I casually strolled through the unit. It was another reminder of just how blessed I was. First, that I was in the physical condition that I was in, but also that my mom was here every day with me from sunup to sundown, giving care, prayer, concern and massages. I'd only been in Atlanta for eight months, so I'd only made a handful of friends there. Though all four of the folks that made up my new Atlanta tribe made their way to the hospital to see me, a dark reality dawned on me: I could've died right here in Atlanta, and it wouldn't have made a bit of a difference to Atlanta and the people in it. As I thanked God for my mom getting here safely and staying with me, that nagging feeling I'd felt so heavily the night before the aneurysm snuck in once again: *You're so far away from home.*

I shook the feeling and focused on taking one step at a time. Halfway through our walk I got a burst of energy as "We're Blessed" by Fred Hammond came up on the rotation. With Nurse K's phone hanging out of my hospital gown pocket, we paused so I could stop and turn up the volume. Moving forward with a slight spring in my step and a jig on my spirit, I began to flex physically as God flexed with me.

Late in the midnight hour!

"Alright now, Jazmine," my mom said from behind the camera, "take it easy."

God's gonna turn it around!

"Don't overwhelm yourself."

And around! And around! And around! And around!

And that He did. Just 96 hours ago I was rolled into Piedmont Atlanta hospital, rushed into emergency surgery with phrases like "unstable and critically ill," "impairment of vital organs," "high probability of imminent/life threatening deterioration," "risks discussed," "stroke, paralysis, blindness, coma, seizures,

41

death," "no guarantees provided," swirling around regarding my condition.

So easily, the results could've been so very different. I could've lost my sight, my ability to walk, my memory, my mind, my sense of self, my life, even. But God saw fit that I not only come out of that operating room alive, but that I'd come out just as I was before. The only difference now is that I came out renewed. Reborn. Refreshed. Rolled out with a new appreciation for life and a heart that beat the same way physically but now, so intensely with purpose that I felt like I was exploding with passion. True to my stage name, Jazz was indeed on fire but now, for God.

I came out seemingly unscathed. There was only a physical scar you couldn't find even if you looked for it. The hair has grown back, the scar has scabbed over, but my faith has grown stronger than ever. I went from near death to a newfound sense of faith, burning with a desire to get to know this God that was so good to me. This miraculous experience so graciously reintroduced me to God, such a merciful and generous Father, who blessed me, saved me and was faithful to me even when I wasn't faithful to Him.

It's a conscious and consistent commitment to give Him a yes every day, and to say no to the things that used to satisfy me. I do it because I was convicted and changed. Sometime during that day when on FaceTime with a fellow life-of-the-party cousin, she told me we'd have to drink to this one when I'm out. Before I could respond, the words came out so fast that they shocked me too.

"Cous', I think I might be putting the bottle down after this one," I said.

And as I said it, I wanted to take it back. Because if I said it, I'd have to stand on it and honor it. I didn't know if I was strong enough to do that. But that's the keyword: *Was.* You just don't know how strong you are until you have no choice but to be and thank God that even in moments where I wasn't and couldn't be, His strength is perfect in my weakness. I took that promise and decided it'd be the first of many sacrifices I'd make to be truly and totally transformed.

We returned to my room after my 15-minute walk of freedom, where I gladly took my oxycodone. I laid awake in bed for a short while before the narcotic began to take its toll. I rode the wave of relief following the surrender, knowing I was so blessed, favored and protected. Sensing a nap coming on, my momma bowed out for a short break where she'd go for coffee and fresh air while I got some rest. As I laid in bed starting to feel the effects of the oxy, I was overwhelmed with gratitude and full of conviction that I could and would never be the same again. And that was okay. That was God's intention.

"Hey Siri, play *'I Won't Go Back'* by William McDowell."

Eyes closed and hand waving, I sang along to the song. Tears streamed down my face as I sang. I felt every single word. Many times, I've called on God during struggle. Or I've made false promises to change while hanging over a toilet and barely hanging onto my consciousness after a night of too much to drink. But this time, I really meant it. This was my second chance, and I intended to get it right. I didn't know all the details, I didn't know the ins and outs or the specifics, but I knew that salvation is a confession, a repentance and a fresh yes. So as the lyrics rang through the room, I gave God my yes that this experience would not be in vain, and that I would not go back to life as I knew it before. And with that spiritual peace falling over me like a warm hospital blanket, I dozed off into a midday nap.

5

Bananas and Chocolate Ensure Shakes

"Cuz' even through inexplicable pain they got jokes, they got joy from me, they got jubilation because I had this crazy faith that told me the battle was already won."

I was never a morning person, but 4 a.m. became my favorite time of the day.

Deep breath in... Exhale.

The early dawn wake up calls became a secret safe haven. It was one of the few moments I could open the shades and remember what outside looked like. Take in the views. Bask in the beauty where speckles of the Atlanta skyline met deep purple skies sprinkled with stars.

Hey Siri, shuffle my playlist 'Praise Break.'

After the nurses would wake me for my early morning round of medicines, I'd stay up to pray and sing while admiring the illuminated skyline outside the window that competed with the colorful medical machinery inside. How funny. Never once when I'd imagined the luxury of skyline views from wraparound floor-to-ceiling windows, did I picture they'd be from the 5th floor of a neuro-intensive care unit at a hospital.

At first, I was extremely disgruntled when they'd wake me for my Q4H doses in the middle of the night. But then I realized how still everything felt. The murmur of machines and the soft buzz of nighttime Atlanta on the not-so-sleepy Peachtree Road below. The hushed whispers of passerby nurses as they whisked from room to room. The fresh, warm blanket laid over me as an incentive for the inconvenience of broken rest. I used to begrudgingly take my meds while still hiding behind my silk sleep mask, quickly shooing away the nurse so I could fall back asleep. But after my body started to catch up on rest during the day from my oxycodone naps, those wake-up calls became a *wake-up call*, where I'd sit at full attention to sing, pray, and talk to God.

Almost losing your life reminds you of just how fragile life can be. So, I took these moments in between lost sleep and lapses in pain to praise God for the 'right then.' Before the aneurysm, my morning devotional to God was limited to less than 15 minutes and truthfully, was spent mostly with me talking and asking. But my morning meet-ups unintentionally became seeds that planted a practice of a deeper, much more intentional devotional. Looking out that window, the world was still, the pain was minimal, and it felt like, once again, God was in the room. I had His undivided attention because He finally had mine. To date, I wake up as the sun rises, sit before my window in the soft morning light and thank God for another chance to do so.

* * *

My mom would waltz in each morning with a selection of goodies from the hospital gift shop in hopes that I could stomach those better than the premade platters from the cafeteria, and to help with all the deficiencies

I was facing from not eating. Bananas—which usually aren't my fruit of choice because of the texture—surprisingly agreed well with my stomach and became a frequent purchase. Sometime in the first week, they had incorporated protein shakes into my diet because I simply could not survive off bananas and assorted hospital cafe candies alone.

"We're going to start you on Ensure since you're struggling to eat solids," the nurse said. "We've got strawberry, vanilla and chocolate, what flavor do you want to try first?"

A strawberry milkshake enthusiast, I opted for the former and sat in lowkey excitement simply because I'd finally wanted to eat something.

After disappearing for a few minutes, she returned empty handed, holding only an apologetic look.

"So, we only have chocolate and vanilla," she said.

"Chocolate it is."

Nurse Mom was already peeling my afternoon banana for me as the nurse placed my room temperature Ensure and a cup of ice on my bedside table.

Ice? With a shake? Have I not gone through enough?

Preparing for it to be one of the worst things I'd ever tasted, I watched in unwarranted disgust and ate my banana as my mom prepped my liquid meal. I was clearing a bite of my banana when she put the straw to my mouth for a sip of long-overdue protein.

Oh. My. Goodness. Why does this taste like Heaven right now?

It could've been delirium from eating very little the past few days, but this

Ensure shake reminded me of something. After motioning for her to bring the cup back for another sip, I realized the familiarity came from the chocolate shake mixing with the banana.

"Ma, this tastes like a banana split!"

Oddly, I was overwhelmed with emotion. I'd only been in the hospital for three days, but 72 hours of bed rest, constant pain, round-the-clock meds and a lack of connection to life outside those four hospital walls makes you feel every single minute of that time. And after struggling to eat and keep food down for three days, we'd found a solution. And it was a solution that reminded me of good times and childhood memories of trips to the Charlie West grill to split ice cream sundaes.

As you can see, the recovery process for a brain bleed isn't the most enjoyable experience.

I initially struggled to eat, stemming from either a general lack of appetite and nausea, or because the pain was so intense that the physical act of chewing was unbearable. As previously discovered, the quality of the pre-order hospital food didn't make it any better. My sodium levels were the furthest thing from stable, prompting the doctors to express sentiments both he and I never thought we'd hear from a doctor:

"Eat as much junk food as you want, we need to up your salt intake."

Because sodium levels closely correlate with fluid in the brain, this needed to be regulated not only for my release, but to prevent further complications and brain damage.

But several times, I felt this unexpected joy from something I never would've bat an eyelash at outside these walls. From the warmth I felt as a cold, Chick-fil-a cookies and cream milkshake made its way down–one of the first solid foods I'd consumed—to the relief that rushed over me when I discovered that grape Ocean Spray juice neutralized the nauseating taste of the twice-a-day salt tabs I was assigned to boost my sodium levels.

It might've been unconventional, but those moments were when God reminded me that I could do this. The first couple of days were the hardest. But once I'd gotten over the lack of appetite and nausea, once the headaches weren't as severe and my medicine schedule gradually transitioned to less often than every 4 hours, my stay became a lot more comfortable.

The doctors warned that headaches would still be present and that they would be bad. While the pain was different than the rupture headache that brought me there, it was a similar intensity. A general soreness would radiate through my entire head, and a pulsating throb comparable to the feeling of a heartbeat at the nape of my neck would cause every nerve in my head to ache. I'd open my mouth allowing my jaw to ride the rhythm of the aching for relief, like a seizure movement that warranted worry and whispered prayers from my mom every single time. The most comparable description of the sensation would be that it felt like my brain was aggressively beatboxing.

I was very blessed that my learning curve wasn't as steep as it could've been. The Lord preserved my mind and memory so that nothing was lost, but I did have some adjusting to do. I had to learn to sneeze properly, as not to throw off the pressure in my brain. I had to learn to wait on the nurses before making sudden movements. Once I could get up and walk to the bathroom again, I had to learn to go a specific way, so I didn't give myself a headache. I had to learn to shift and hold my jaw in the perfect position to keep the throbbing at bay when the headaches were bad. I had to learn to breathe through the needles and smile through the pain.

* * *

It felt like the day I took my first stroll outside the room flipped a switch. I'd been bedridden by force, but once I had the power to get up, it was past time to walk into my healing. With the introduction of standing and walking, though still under the supervision of a nurse, I now had the freedom to sit in the chair or physically get up and go to the bathroom if I could call a nurse and make it on time. Getting out of bed felt like more than *just* getting out of bed. It reminded me of that moment back at the apartment where I'd decided to get up off that couch and go to the hospital. Getting out of bed was my declaration that I wouldn't be holed up and held down. I declared that I would fight through this thing with everything in me. Back and leg pain had to bow to the name of Jesus who was so obviously strengthening me.

My first solid meal later that week was a 10-piece chicken nugget combo from Wendy's with a cheddar baked potato. I sat propped up in my bedside chair, warm rag covering my eyes, legs elevated with a pillow underneath, head back in preparation for another broken nugget. I'd chew hungrily but gently, as not to agitate my brain that was momentarily calm enough for me to eat. I couldn't get enough. After a few days of eating just enough to get the nurses off my back, I finally felt normal–and hungry–enough to eat and enjoy the taste of food. It felt amazing. Each bite of Wendy's felt gourmet, and alternating bites of baked potato and chicken nugget became a slice of solace; a comfort food that can still bring me an uncommon level of joy.

"Girl, you killed those," my momma said as she shook the almost empty nugget box, "it's only two left."

What was that I noticed in her voice? Was she proud?

I remember the years in grade school constantly wanting to make my momma proud. But endless awards ceremonies and academic achievements couldn't compare to the feeling I felt as my momma looked on at me, beaming with joy, for almost finishing a 10-piece nugget. I watched her watch me all day, constantly staring in concern, waiting and worrying, pulling on her strength as she'd hurt with me too. But satisfaction radiated from her as she spoon-fed her 23-year-old daughter scoops of baked potato and broken nugget portions. In my surrender, I was able to show her she didn't need to worry either.

As I wrapped up my meal, I sat on the chair suddenly feeling a familiar tiredness: my old friend, the 'itis! I'd barely eaten enough the past few days to fill my stomach to take all my medicine, and here I was today, feeling full, content and a few deep breaths away from a food-induced nap. Little wins like this were when I realized God's weight was crushing recovery, causing me to breeze through it.

The nurse was not kidding when she said recovery would be no easy feat. There was so much pain, discomfort, challenges, and mountains ahead of me that it would've been easy to be discouraged.

But there was always something that kept me going. Cold compresses and hot rags became a holy grail. Bananas and chocolate Ensure shakes, and grape Ocean Spray and salt tab combinations became a saving grace. *My Wife and Kids* on cable was a glimmer of light shining through a long, dark tunnel. Tubes of Curad petroleum jelly to fight chapped lips and realizing that I could customize my cafeteria orders were the perfect pick-me-ups. These little things, these subtle things, reminded me that sickness was not my story, and that even amidst my situation, joy was possible.

Joy was also contagious, as I'd befriend every nurse and technician that came in.

"Girl, I need to talk to whoever you got praying for you because MY GOD," said the male nurse, who had no problem during my stay reminding me how in awe he was at my recovery.

"Oh, this is the party room right here," another nurse said as she entered, two-stepping to the gospel music I constantly had playing on my Alexa.

From phone calls with loved ones, visits from my very few, new local friends, to bringing in pieces of home to make me more comfortable, like my Alexa, a bonnet, deep conditioner, and deodorant—which I'd realized I hadn't been given in a few days—several things brought me joy in the hospital.

Warm blankets, new fuzzy socks that fit my small feet, mesh medical underwear, milkshakes, gift shop candy bags, bananas and chocolate ensure shakes, using the toilet, fresh sheets and bed pads. I'd found the rainbows within all the pain and sunk into a comfortable routine in such an uncomfortable situation. The more I walked in my joy, the easier it came. The more I believed in my healing, the more real it became.

The day after I took my first walk around the unit was followed by the removal of the IVD. They swapped my brain drain tube for the remote that reclined the bed. With that came more freedom, I could sit up or lay back on my own without calling a nurse. This allowed me to simply adjust if I was uncomfortable, rather than having to wait for a nurse to do so or rough it out when I didn't want to be a bother. The back and tailbone pain from bed rest was exchanged for cool lidocaine patches in the morning that worked wonders, reminiscent of that crisp feeling in your mouth when you drink ice water while chewing gum. Once I laid my internal worries down and exchanged them for prayer, all my exterior problems were exchanged for solutions. God continued to top Himself every day. By the end of the first week, I started to feel normal again with just a little Tylenol and a good night's rest. No nausea, no drowsiness from medication, no lingering aches or pressure headaches the moment I woke up. I felt like myself. It was a beautiful feeling to wake up pain free, one I treasure dearly every day.

We were watching Ebeneezer's live Sunday service when a new nurse with a peculiar-looking silver tool entered the room. It was a frightening mash-up of scissors, a finger-nail clipper and a handheld hole-puncher. I had an inkling of exactly what that tool would be used for.

"Alright Miss Bunch, we're going to remove those staples," she said.

Fear quickly put my excitement in a headlock as I realized what that meant. I was out for the 'going in.' But now, I'm wide awake and not ready to experience how this was about to feel.

"You sure y'all can't put me back to sleep for this?"

The nurse, my mom and stepdad Gerald, who'd arrived in Atlanta the night before, erupted into laughter. I swallowed the lump in my throat and forced a half smile as I was, unfortunately, very serious about my question. Seven staples, with each becoming a little more uncomfortable than the last since some of them had started to scab over and my hair began to grow back. I wiped the tears that reactively welled in my eyes as she pulled the last one out of place.

"WHEW."

Talk about never wanting to feel that again. But it was over. Another mountain I'd never imagined I'd have to climb, but I made it to the other side. I was advised on the best way to clean the areas and signs to watch for infection as the surgery sites healed. I'd had two linear scars leading to a circle area from the burr hole where the tube was draining the fluid. I shuddered and shook the thought, charging it to be a not-right-now problem. We continued to watch the service, as the "we gon' be alright" theme transformed into a full, virtual production.

I *was* alright. Here I was, standing in a promise that just last week I had no choice but to hope in. Today I was walking in it. I was so much better than just alright. God was showing out with me, bringing me over my mountain faster than the doctors could explain. I had an appetite again. I was going to the bathroom on my own. The only pain I was experiencing was area sensitivity due to laughing at FaceTime calls from friends and at Nurse Mom, who'd become a lot lighter.

When vasospasms became the least of our worries, vanity came and plopped right in the forefront.

"I look a mess! Can you please bring my scarf from the house?"

"Jazmine, you are not supposed to be putting anything on your head," my mom objected.

We coined her Nurse Mom early into the week because from giving massages, to bedside baths, to wiping down the room and disinfecting tools, to advising what I should and shouldn't do, you would've sworn she was one of my nurses. The joke became especially funny the morning she walked into the room, dressed in her usual sweatpants, t-shirt and navy-blue walking sneakers. But this time, she was decked out head to toe in hospital blue.

"Girl, I thought you were a nurse for real," I said before erupting into laughter. "What do you have on there? You think you're a nurse for real, don't you?"

She looked down at her outfit and it quickly dawned on her that she came to the hospital dressed like a nurse for the day. We laughed for too long at the joke as she began to tell me about the outer hospital happenings that entertained her during her trips outside. The emergency room was perched on the bustling Peachtree Road, sandwiched between Buckhead and Midtown, so there would surely be some action. She'd reenact the random goings-on she encountered during her quick expeditions outside, and we'd laugh until our stomachs hurt and I begged her to stop.

I'm sure she reveled in those moments where we could exchange groans of pain for giggles and trade shut-eyed head pain for laughter-induced stomach cramps. I don't know how I would've done it without her. God knew I needed my momma there with me. So, there she was every single day. Worry aside, fear of traffic out the window, walking just as confidently as I was in this God-given assurance that I would be okay.

By the halfway point in my stay, I'd practically made myself at home. My Alexa was in the room and connected to the Wi-Fi to help battle the confinement of bed rest when I was alone. My hair was semi-moisturized and detangled, laying underneath the bonnet carefully situated around the surgery site, per Nurse Mom's orders. I was back in charge of my cell phone. When I wasn't resting, I was being entertained via FaceTime by some of my favorite people who hadn't missed a beat praying for and pouring into me. I'd finally begun to be at peace with taking each day as its own, one day at a time. I wasn't in fear of the future and whether my life would go back to normal, because I knew that after this experience, it was intentional that I'd never be the same.

I settled into my situation and didn't allow my diagnosis to dictate my outlook. I continued to wake up before the city did to chop it up with God. I gave the nurses and doctors the best of me. I basked in the joys of my uncommon combinations and even more in how good my God was raining uncommon favor on me. My stay in the neuro-ICU can be described as one full of grit, tears, prayers, needles, medicine, fighting, resting, nightmares, pain, and recovery. But it was also full of devotion, reflection, rest, and relationship with the Father who so graciously carried me through this experience.

6

Revelation

"See if you ask me I was never wheeled through the hallways of a hospital, I was carried through this battle by God's Grace."

In the beginning, I had a really difficult time adjusting to doing nothing.

I didn't realize when the nurses said, "Call me if you need anything." that meant any little thing because I literally wasn't supposed to move an inch without them. One morning early on into my stay, while attempting to do something very simple, a friendly white male nurse who I don't recall seeing again swooped in to take over. I remember adjusting the new PureWick he'd gotten for me as he rolled my bedside table closer and proceeded with his tasks.

"You're used to doing everything on your own, huh?" He said with a chuckle.

Uh, yeah? Doesn't everybody pee on their own?

I forced a drawn-out "Yeah?" and a slight chuckle, a little confused and mildly annoyed at such an obvious statement. It didn't hit me until months later when I was behind the wheel for the first time in months and heard his voice ring in my head: *"You're used to doing things on your own."*

Oh. That's what that was.

A fresh, heavy revelation. I was used to doing things alone, like going to the bathroom and getting out of bed. But also like "life." Like moving to Atlanta and trying to make it feel like home without finding a house of worship. Or spending my days venting to friends about how alone I felt when my Forever Friend was always nearby, waiting to be tagged into the conversation. Like trying to "walk off" a literal brain bleed like it was a strained ankle.

I don't know if I didn't realize it was okay to use my help or failed to realize I had it. The first few days in the hospital were filled with apologies as I learned to surrender control to the plethora of personnel whose livelihood revolved around taking care of me. Now imagine the revelation that fell over me when I realized I stared God in the face, just in the form of a six-foot white man in blue scrubs, gently reminding me that He is, has been, and always will be here to do just that. A gentle reminder of one of the many things this entire experience is supposed to teach me: How to surrender to Him.

I'd been wrestling with being alone in Atlanta when all this time, I was never alone. He brought me here, miraculously having a job advertisement appear on Google for a company where I'd been denied internships numerous times. He showed up in a very affordable, safe—even luxury—living arrangement after searching the market for months and being discouraged that my entry level salary wouldn't be enough to support the cost of living in Georgia.

Despite all this evidence of God working in my life, I constantly mulled over how alone and far away from home I was. I was so hyper-focused on how I was doing everything independently when the revelation was that this was the only way God would have me realize it was never *just* me. It was never me at all. It was always Him. From growing up in a family of six and gaining recognition in my hometown. Countless awards and accolades I brought to—and home from—my schools. Graduating high school as valedictorian. Being the first in my family to attend college. Graduating debt-free. Making it out of my hometown. It was never me, it was always Him. And here I was, with the audacity to be living in Atlanta struggling, crying and trying to figure out life post-college in a new city "on my own" like the Author of my story wasn't waiting to write a supporting cast into my next chapter.

The nurse's words might've fallen on deaf ears then, but they became a word from the Lord that I constantly steeped my walk of faith in moving forward. Though I was used to doing things alone, this moment showed me just how incapable I was of doing things on my own, and how ready God was to step in when I let Him. I didn't save myself, God did. I saw exactly what happened when I tried to fight the headaches alone without the help of the medicine. It made me think about the bigger picture: Why try to fight the headaches of the world on my own when I have a supernatural supplement to fight them for me?

* * *

I was informed from the beginning that my stay in the neuro-ICU would be at least 14 days. My miraculous strides made me optimistic but still focused on healing. But by day 10, I was feeling so much like myself that I started leaning on that 14-day promise and began the countdown.

Just a few more days, the docs said I'll be leaving here on the 17th!

That was the good news I told everyone who called for an update. If God was getting me through it, He could get me out of this hospital.

The nurses would typically write the day's date on the whiteboard—except for the couple of days where no one did, and I thought it was Thursday for two days–so I generally didn't have to keep track of the day or date. I now realize that with bed rest comes the illusion that the day or time was whatever they told me it was. But after a random conversation two days before my scheduled release, I finally made the association that "a few more days", the 17th, and this Sunday were all Easter Sunday.

No freaking way I just realized this.

I was going to be released from my 14-day stay in the neuro-intensive care unit, after miraculously surviving and recovering from a ruptured brain aneurysm on the day in Christianity known as the resurrection of our Lord and Savior. I couldn't believe it. The idea that I was being released on Easter Sunday felt so massive and so important, but I couldn't wrap my head around that it was anything more than a coincidence. So, I took to Instagram to make a joke of it.

"Not I'm scheduled to be released from the hospital on Easter Sunday?! Let me go ahead and get my metaphors popping, the saints gon' have a field day with this one!" I said, alongside a meme featuring a young girl with a pleasantly bemused expression.

But the intentional God I serve absolutely couldn't let me miss my moment of major revelation.

This was the first post I'd made firsthand about my stay in the hospital on Instagram. The only information on social media regarding my condition was in the GoFundMe description posted by my friends. With that, I'm sure those who weren't immediate friends or family who may have been worried, or wondering were anxious to get an update from the horse's mouth.

But the responses flooded in with an overwhelming amount of support. They comically mimicked a twenty-first century version of reactions to the original resurrection if social media existed.

"My [redacted] rising on the sabbath! It's written."
  "It's giving resurrection."
  "OMG. That's actually really powerful, Jazz."
  "You better be reborn, girl!"

With that comment, I was certain this was no coincidence. I was supposed to see this experience exactly as it was… a rebirth. I'd been throwing around the term because it was the only way I could describe how I felt physically coming from under the anesthesia after surgery. It was the only way to explain the new gratitude and devotion to God, whom I'd suddenly felt so close to. Rebirth was the only way to understand how and why I was still here when so many things should've marked the end of my story. With that word, I hopped on FaceTime with Gwen, my unofficial PR agent and my favorite creative thought partner, and we began fleshing out how in the world I would translate this grand revelation into a grand spoken word piece.

The creative juices began flowing before I could get off the phone with her. Before I knew it, my iPhone notes app was filled with fragmented lines, incomplete thoughts and ideas underneath the title "Reborn." We game-planned a "press conference" via the live function on social media, where I'd share my story and the hopefully completed poem on my release day, and she released me to finish writing for our unofficial post-hospital campaign. But there was no need for hope when the God who formed the Heavens and the Earth's creative grace flowed through my veins.

"Sit back for a bit and honey, I'll tell you exactly how it feels to be God's favorite…"

My fingers couldn't keep up with the creative genius flowing out of me. It was almost as if I wasn't writing it, but simply regurgitating a powerful message already written. My writing process typically consists of bouncing around an untitled piece, fleshing out ideas as they come randomly and out of order.

But with this piece, there's not a shadow of a doubt in my mind that God was guiding the pen.

"I feel like Kanye right now. This gotta be how Kanye felt writing My Beautiful Dark Twisted Fantasy," I frantically sent mid-poem to a few of my fellow Kanye appreciators.

I was 10 days removed from a brain bleed, emergency surgery, and an EVD drain. Yet, there I was writing and memorizing one of my most personal and powerful spoken word poems, draped in a hospital gown and tethered to medical machines inside a neuro-intensive care unit. I said it when I posted the video on Instagram, but I still feel so strongly that I was merely a vessel for the piece that later became *Testimony II*. Just like with my story, God was the author.

* * *

I woke up at my usual unusually early time, energized by knowing exactly what day it was: Sunday, April 17th. Easter Sunday. Release day!

The last few days of my stay, I'd received permission from the nurses to go to the bathroom alone, but still only when they were in the room. I carefully sprung out of bed the minute a nurse gave me the go-ahead to use the bathroom and prepare myself for the day.

I exchanged pleasantries with the nurse in the room from the bathroom over the gospel music on my phone. My mom and stepdad were on their way to the hospital. While they made a pit stop for breakfast, I thought I'd try to apply product and twist my hair without the cautious eye of Nurse Mom advising against it.

While it was rare for me not to be, I was on a different level of high spirits this morning. 14 days is a long time when you factor in the bedrest and resulting back pain, medical mattress, hospital food, nightmares, needles, PureWicks, monitored bathroom breaks and bedside baths. Some days, I couldn't even remember life outside of this routine, and I'd settle deeper into the cycle, comforted that all I had to do was trust God. On other days, I worried I was getting too comfortable. But today was the last day, and the promise of peeing by myself and sleeping in my own bed was enough to make me throw the familiarity of my new routine to the wind.

I returned to my bedside chair, patiently waiting for my folks to walk through the door with my chicken, egg and cheese biscuit. I had an appetite again, passed stool properly, wasn't over-excreting my liquid intake, and my sodium levels had finally fallen and remained within a range safe for discharge. One of my favorite nurse techs I hadn't seen in a few days came into the room to collect my vitals and blood sugar. In our conversation, I'd casually mentioned how excited I was to be released today, to which she instantly gave me a look I did not want to see.

"...or am I not?" I said, trying to swallow the gigantic lump of disappointment welling up.

"...Umm, Doc hasn't mentioned anything to me," she started delicately, "But I can go ask to make sure."

All I could rally up was an "aww." Surprisingly, with all the dire diagnoses, this was probably the first time I outwardly expressed disappointment. It felt warranted. I took all the medicine. I took all the needles. I took it easy. I gathered all my strength to do whatever was needed to improve my health. I was patient all 13 other days and there seemed to be no reason why I couldn't leave today as promised. There was no indication that I wouldn't be, so I was crushed.

What about the metaphor? Or my and Gwen's unofficial release campaign? I was supposed to be rising like Jesus! Nothing was spectacular or symbolic about being released on Monday, April 18th!

And as I mitigated the very unserious PR crisis swirling through my head, the nurse tech interrupted with a valid thought.

"The doctor just wants to make sure you're good on release so that you won't have to come back here, you know?"

I put out the PR fires in my head and realized that was probably a very good point. I did not want to leave this hospital with anything that'd bring me back. I settled into the ever-so-familiar bedside chair accepting I would occupy room 5A-2 for another day. My momma and stepdad came in soon after, and she instantly picked up on my disappointment.

"Well Jazmine, I know you'd rather leave here knowing everything is all good, so you don't have to come back," she said.

"Yeah, I know, I know," I grumbled as I turned on Ebenezer's 9 a.m. Easter Sunday service right in time to catch the full-scale music video of their "We Gon' Be Alright" gospel-rap remix. I had no choice in staying here another day, but I had a choice in being happy about it. Rather than sitting in frustration or disappointment for the rest of the day, I figured I might as well rejoice and be glad I was still here to even see it.

But first, I had to send my rounds of responses to the people sending encouraging release day texts.

Gwen was the first I'd break the news to, as our carefully crafted release day shenanigans wouldn't quite work anymore.

"And on this day Jazmine rose from the porcelain hospital room as Jesus did from his stone grave," the text read.

"Unfortunately, I'm not going home today," I responded.

A quick—and once again, very unserious—exchange ensued regarding the "looks" of it from a PR standpoint, with the conversation ending on a *"Jazmine... please just trust me on this ok,"* and a mildly annoyed Jazmine who refused to respond.

I continued the Easter service while finishing my sandwich, still trying to accept that I'd spend another day in Piedmont Atlanta Hospital.

Dr. P popped in for his usual rounds of mental tests and medical assessments.

"Everything's looking pretty good, Miss Bunch," he said as he clicked off his penlight.

A simple phrase I'd grown so fond of hearing.

Not good enough to leave today though.

I worried I mistakenly voiced my grumpy thoughts out loud as he immediately followed up with sympathy.

"If it was up to me, you'd be able to leave, but it's essentially the surgeon's call."

I gave him a nod of understanding as he left the room, with him bidding promises that it should be no later than tomorrow. My family and I continued to listen to the service from my cell phone until Dr. S appeared at the door not long after.

"I got some good news," he began. "You're leaving"
   "Tomorrow?" I said.
   "Today."

"TODAY?"

"Today."

"STOP," I managed to squeeze out before the waterworks kicked in.

For whatever reason, though I tried hard to deny it, a tiny part of me was afraid of leaving the hospital. Even after all God had done and how much I'd recovered, I thought I'd never leave. Though disappointed on the surface, part of me was oddly comforted when I first learned I wasn't getting out. But this was the final call from the man with say-so, so I knew it was real. I wouldn't dare admit it then, but there was a hint of worry mixed in with those happy tears.

My momma and stepdad chuckled as I wiped my face, and Dr. S excused himself to alert the nurses to get a jumpstart on my discharge. The 'rents excused themselves shortly after my mom packed up the last of my things before beginning the trek across the hospital to get the car pulled around front. One of my earlier nurses from the first few days was back. In a full circle moment, Nurse Z and I discussed life pre-aneurysm and post-Piedmont. She began the convoluted process of untethering me from my myriad of monitors, a gentle apology following each uncomfortable removal of an EKG patch. She scrubbed with alcohol all the stubborn spots of residue left from the electrodes and days of medical tape holding IVs in place, advising a routine of this to help wear out the sticky souvenirs that apparently would be going home with me. The sticky stragglers–I could handle taking home, but the opioid-level drugs were where I drew the line.

"Do you want a prescription to take with you for the oxy?" she asked.

It took quite a bit of convincing for me to hop on the oxy train in my earlier days, and even once on it, I took the ride carefully. The nurses constantly cautioned me that the headaches wouldn't just go away and even assured me they'd be normal for my condition. But the God I serve allowed me to experience relief from the alleged lingering headaches before even leaving the hospital–in the final few days without the help of the opioids. If that was any indication, I knew I'd be fine without them.

"Okay, you're fine to take two 500 mg Tylenols for headaches," she said.

"Your veins are sensitive from the IVs, so no lifting anything heavier than a jug of milk for the rest of the day."

"No driving for two weeks."

"Headaches are normal, but if something doesn't feel normal, call 9-1-1."

"The doctor requested you see your primary care doctor to check your sodium levels no later than a week from today."

I changed clothes as she continued running down the list of things to watch out for, avoid and to begin that were also listed in my discharge packet. We'd gotten to the stroke acronym section of Discharge-101 when it truly settled on me that the past two weeks were some of the most life-changing days I'd ever experienced.

...F is for face drooping; A is arm weakness or tingling...

And the rest of my life would truly never be the same.

...S is speech and difficulty speaking...

Freedom welled over me as I'd put on an actual pair of cotton underwear for the first time in 2 weeks.

...T means time to call 9-1-1...

The hospital gown dropped to my ankles. I stepped out of my grave clothes and into one of my favorite comfy dresses. Removing that pale, blue hospital gown, which did nothing for my skin, felt like a symbol of freedom. As long as I'd had on that gown, I felt bound to this condition—these conditions—shackled under the mental anguish that accompanied being a "patient." But no more. I felt free. No more polyester chains and twill tape ties holding me.

I untwisted my semi-damp hair and accepted the last bit of the nurse's help to put on my sneakers.

I wrote personal thank you cards for all my nurses and surgeons. I'd distributed most of them through the morning and the night prior, so I kept an eye out to catch as many as possible to personally hand it to them before I was officially discharged. With the ability to freely roam through the hallways, I could hunt down the remaining nurses, with Nurse P, the first face I'd woken up to, as the last to be found. Although I was masked, she instantly knew it was me as I approached her.

"Well look at you!" she said.

I did a slight bow, because well, duh, and blushed as she looked on in awe. We exchanged sentiments of admiration and I let her know that I included my Instagram handle for us to connect if she was allowed to.

As I walked through the hallways delivering thank you cards, it felt like a scene from a Hallmark movie. Nurses and personnel who'd either taken care of me or who'd witnessed any part of my recovery clapped for me or expressed awe as I walked by. Thankfully, a nurse offered to take my picture underneath the Neuro-ICU sign in the hallway. As I returned to the door of 5A-2 to be accompanied by Nurse Z to the pick-up area, I gave them a Jazz finale, the last joke of the stay.

"Y'all were amazing but I never wanna see y'all again!" I said as they erupted into laughter.

Nurse Z handed me my discharge papers and we did a final scan of the room to ensure nothing was left behind.

"It's kind of far, do you want a wheelchair, or do you think you feel okay to walk?" she asked.

I was a little warm and winded from my Easter nurse hunt around the unit but requested to walk without hesitation. I was rolled into Piedmont Atlanta's emergency room 14 days prior on Sunday, April 3rd. I was in an inexplicable amount of pain. Body seizing, light blinding, spine stiffening and unable to just lie still for an MRI. I was rushed into emergency endovascular coiling for a brain bleed. Sunday, April 17th, I walked out of that hospital.

So many times, by so many people I was called a walking miracle, and now it was officially my time to walk in it.

As we trekked through the hospital halls, she explained how we took a route a lot shorter and less convoluted than the one my parents, my mom especially, took alone every single day. As we walked through long stretches of halls and brief elevator rides down, I tried to imagine what it must have been like for her the first time my mom took this route. I imagined the anxiety building with each stride, fear growing in each step after an eight-hour ride and such dire news. I imagined how it felt walking through this maze of a hospital that night, and every single morning, not knowing what exactly she'd see the next time she laid eyes on me. I shook the feeling of heaviness. I'd walked in faith, not fear, my entire stay in the neuro-ICU, so it was only right that I decided to leave that emotional heaviness here as well.

As we exited the final elevator, we'd walked past the gift shop and hospital cafe my mom frequented for her morning coffee and my cafe goodies. We rounded the corner to the large open entrance where I noticed my mom was recording on her phone from across the hospital. I threw up the peace sign and did a two-step for the camera before Nurse Mom stopped the party with her favorite new phrase; "take it easy."

I bid my goodbyes to Nurse Z and waited for Gerald to pull the car around.

As I saw my black Honda turn into the circular entrance of the hospital's pick-up area, I flipped my camera on for a POV to my feet as I slowly rose from the seat. My momma wasn't too far behind, shooting me a quick "you okay?" to which I replied with a confident "mhm," and began to walk forward, capturing my steps toward the opening automatic glass doors of the hospital. I quickly swapped to the front facing camera and tossed up the peace sign with a glimpse of the hospital in the background.

"Let me out, let me out, Happy Easter!"

My mom helped me into the backseat to make sure I didn't bump my head getting in. I fastened my seatbelt, settled into the seat and took a deep breath as we pulled out of the web of roads leading to and from the hospital's emergency entrance. As we pulled onto Peachtree Road, I realized I knew exactly where I was and began associating momma's wild stories of Peachtree Road happenings with the various shops we passed by. There was the Chick-fil-A the nurses frequented for lunch breaks. There's the Yumbii where I unexpectedly had the best Korean fried chicken, and the CVS where my mom purchased my pack of thank-you cards. I rested my head on the seat and stared out the window, watching the glass tower of Piedmont Atlanta whiz by in the distance as a song rose in my spirit.

I am free, Praise the Lord, I am free. No longer bound, no more chains holding me. My soul is resting, it's just a blessing. Praise the Lord. Hallelujah, I'm free.

7

Seven Weeks in Spring

There's something so satisfying about the smell and feel of a brand-new hardcover book. The vivid blues and pinks of Tia Williams" *Seven Days In June* cover jumped out as I flipped through the pages to waft the aroma. I sent a thank-you text to my friend, Anissa, for the care package while reveling in the smell.

A love story, I thought to myself, *how fitting.*

I thought it'd be beautiful to read this fictional love story as my own unfolded.

I admit that our mutual love for reading incentivized me to free-read again. I was so excited to have another thing to share with him besides our weekly watch parties perched in front of Peacock watching Bel-Air.

I remember the first day I saw him. He was a candidate among a catalog of digital faces.

Cute, but not really my type. I'll go on the date anyway. He's cute enough.

I remember the first day we met: Light brown skin against yellow, the first of many times that seeing him would remind me of sunshine. I was right, he was cuter in person.

We met shortly after Valentine's Day. Every minute I'd spent with him since the first felt like Cupid was pulling overtime to personally grant me my never-ending version. He was handsome, kind, goal-oriented, chivalrous and we had so much in common. He made me feel comfortable and safe. He checked all the boxes. He was perfect. *This* was perfect. For the first time—like, ever—there were no red flags.

If you're confused at why it's February 2022 and I'm perfectly healthy and head-over-heels for someone's son, I promise we'll get there. Stick it out with me.

We spent increasingly more time together after the first date, starting our weekly Peacock watch parties and reserving the evenings after work for romantic outings exploring the city of Atlanta together. He was from Georgia, but he'd recently moved closer to the city and still had some exploring to do. But this was his home, and he'd started to make it feel like that for me too.

This was my first healthy, adult relationship, so I was nervous but open. After a series of flings, failures, and forget-me-pleases in college, I began this personal journey of spiritual and emotional self-preservation. I was so deep in the "my-body-is-a-temple" bag that I felt at peace with being single for so long. So, I approached Valentine's Day very single, but content. I was on this beautiful wave of accepting that I was in alignment with whatever and whoever God had for me. So, right when I accepted that I would spend yet another love day alone, love walked in.

After binge-watching the first four available episodes of Bel-Air one evening soon after our first date, we sat and talked for hours about everything from our careers to goals, family, and the future. We sat perpendicular to each other across his uncomfortable sectional. I was wrapped in his arms, his heartbeat reverberating in my ear and the gentle vibration of his speech radiating through his chest as he spoke. It was one of those conversations where you lost track of time. One of those moments straight from a romance novel. Here I was in this new city, this new life, in this decreasingly new person's arms, but I felt safe. I felt free to root. To melt. We set boundaries, we talked about intentions, we discussed love languages, we reflected on the past, and set our eyes on the future. It was a great night, so great that it was hard to leave. But I left feeling warm and filled, knowing that I was going to trust the God that brought me here to take me through it, whatever "it" was going to be.

We spent what I considered to be a healthy amount of time together, even as that time increased. I was adamant about allowing myself to be open and soft, and he made the space for it, allowing me to do so. It was perfect. For so long, I wondered if there was a person for me, or if I'd even be properly dated like other women in their 20s and experience what it felt like to truly be courted, cared for and protected. Everything I'd been praying for was happening, and everything I stopped allowing and doing to make space for this was worth it. Which is why I was terrified about having the conversation about abstinence.

We'd been having such a good time genuinely getting to know each other and enjoying each other's company that the thought hadn't even crossed my mind. We shared space, were close, and were intimate, but it was never sensual. We hadn't even kissed yet. I appreciated the pacing of it, it was so refreshing. It felt like 'building something,' not just rushing into something to close the door behind us and remove our clothes. But I felt like there was a need to make sure that I liked him before there was even a need to bring up sex, or the absence of it. And after talking with my therapist, who'd been a great sounding board through this entire "soft girl" process, it was decided that since things seemed to be getting serious, it was important that a conversation happened soon. One night while we were snuggled up on that small, uncomfortable sectional, I mustered my courage, which physically translated to very noticeable shallow breaths.

"You okay?" he asked.

Shoot, I thought.

Now or never. I fumbled a half-question, half-statement as ungracefully as possible, which caused the need for even more of an explanation on my part. I can't remember how it came out, but my heart raced as I couldn't translate whether his confusion was irritation or a genuine need for clarity. So, I just said it.

"I'm abstinent. And I want to stay abstinent…for a while."

I explained why, because I felt comfortable enough to do so. To be transparent, it wasn't completely based on religion at the time. I'd gained a new perspective on the "my body is a temple" mantra, so the purpose was steeped in personal conservation rather than holy sanctification. But every tense muscle relaxed when his reaction wasn't to immediately throw me out of his apartment. Instead, he looked me in my eyes and told me he'd wait with me. Like me, he was having such a good time enjoying my company that it wasn't top of mind. And just like that, the only possible red flag left to be discovered was washed away in the wave of relief that flooded over me. *God, you really did send him, huh?*

After that night, I gave myself permission–not to fall–but to step out on faith. To be extremely open to this experience of being loved properly. To be respected, cared for, adored, showered in compliments and flowers. There were museums, food dates, open mic nights, book swaps, movie nights in, sharing secrets, evening drives, sleepovers, meeting friends, nonsexual intimacy, forehead kisses before leaving for work in the morning, *I'll pick my key up on my way in from work,* the day he told me he loved me.

We were moving fast, but in a good way. I didn't have a baseline to compare it to because this was my first true adult relationship. Still, I accepted that about two months' worth of experiences and time together warranted something deeper than "I really care about you." It wasn't forced, it wasn't expected. It came amidst a conversation the morning after a night of a few too many drinks and too little space. I was deep in my mild, lemon pepper seafood boil when the words at the end of a long, sentimental message came in and took my breath away.

"...Like I love you, so we can move as slow as you want or at whatever pace makes you feel comfortable, it's all good."

"Wait, you love me?"

"Yeah, this has exceeded just liking you. I love you."

I immediately panicked and called my friends.

"Y'ALL, DID HE JUST SAY WHAT I THINK HE SAID?!"

"Yep."
   "Girl, he sure did."
   "OMG!"

"Is it too early? Do I say it back? OMG, what do I do?"

Was it too early? Do I love him? At this point, it had only been a month since we started dating but we were spending a lot of time together. I did care for him deeply, and I loved him being around.

But I needed to be sure. We were draped across his bed a few nights later singing along to 2000s lyric videos. I took a moment while the ad in between songs played in the background.

"So," I began, "you like, love me?"

Very graceful.

"I do," he said without missing a beat.

"But like, how do you know?" I asked. "You haven't even seen every side of me to know that. Like when I'm impatient, angry, sad, or moody."

I recently saw a post defining love as seeing someone in every emotion and stage and feeling the same about them regardless. I decided to adopt that for myself.

"I've seen enough of you to know that I'll love you in those moments too," he said.

My heart swelled and I truly did try to gain control of my tear ducts. But this unofficial "for better or worse" solidified that I was living in an answered prayer: To experience what it felt like to be loved the way I desired.

When we were younger, there was always this crazy pressure around those three words; how and when they're said, if it's said a specific way, who says it first. But he said them first, so there was no pressure on my end. And with the opportunity to take it back but not doing so, I assumed he must've meant it. I know how I felt, and how he made me feel. How effortless it felt to love him and for me to feel loved. This felt safe, easy, and healthy–I did love him. I was glad I said it back over my salty seafood boil. And that was it. I guess we loved each other.

* * *

After sharing the latest love life updates with my therapist, I had to get serious. I loved how authentic and open I could be with her. I was intentional about finding a black woman therapist, so our sessions felt like talking to a close girlfriend with an informed, expert opinion.

"Okay girl, so give me the tea. Am I being love bombed?" I asked seriously after reveling in the romantics. "I don't know how this works. Is it too early?"

I was intentional about healthily balancing on the tightrope of not convincing myself that this was too good to be true, while letting myself walk in the delusion that maybe it was. She was there too, right by my side assuring me of the other possibility that maybe it just was that good and that I deserved it.

"So, the question is… will you be okay if it isn't?" she asked.

I took a second to honestly discern the answer to that question. I was careful this time that while I let the walls down and gave it my all, I didn't give it all to the point where I'd feel only emptiness if he left.

"Yes, I will be," I said confidently.

* * *

"Okay, I just finished *Seven Days in June* and can't wait for you to read it," I said. "I will warn you, though, it gets pretty steamy."

I was so excited to hear his thoughts on the book. I loved his mind. I loved hearing his thoughts and how he felt about me, the world and our story. Tia Williams was such a beautiful writer and eloquent storyteller. My inner creative leapt and jumped at the thought of sharing this love story of hers while creating our own. So, we did.

He would read chunks of the book and we'd debrief. I already felt like I was over the moon, and things continued to get sweeter. We continued to build, get to know each other, go on dates, and have our recurring binge-watching parties. I always try to be realistic, but I was allowing myself to settle into this fairytale. I remember the first night we had our heart-to-heart on that uncomfortable sectional of his. I told him how this past Valentine's Day, I was just happy to see other black women getting loved on and his response was, *"yeah, and now you're one of them."* I was elated. Content. Secure. In a loving, growing relationship that I allowed myself to be in. I was being showered in love, affections, promises and affirmations. Things were perfect.

Until the aneurysm, when I guess they just weren't perfect enough for him to stay.

Funny enough, I set a boundary that he wouldn't know where I lived or be able to enter my space until I felt the timing was right. One evening early in our relationship, I was cooking dinner to take to his place and nearly chopped my finger clean off while slicing a lemon. I was struggling to stop the bleeding. Since Kennedy wasn't home and my other friend, Maia, wasn't available, I texted him and told him I might need him to take me to the hospital. He instantly called me for my address. Although the amount of blood shooting from my finger was concerning, the urgency in his voice as I heard him shuffling to get to me was so comforting. I ended up giving in and allowing him to help me. Even if I was able to stop the bleeding, I wouldn't be able to finish cooking with only nine and a half fully functional fingers. He came over and helped me to stop the bleeding, clean the cut and bandaged me up. But I didn't learn until after I was properly bandaged that he wasn't a fan of blood. How sweet? To know that he put my needs over his discomfort. He was such a caretaker, and I'd experience this urgency a few more times. Which is why I was so taken aback this time, when it really mattered, he didn't show up.

This part of the story is difficult to tell because I still struggle to accept it.

It was April 1st, and we planned a summer trip back to my hometown. April 2nd came, and we discussed upcoming spring break plans: Amusement parks, drive-in zoos, movie theater dates, days in the house binge-watching a new shared series.

The morning of April 3rd, we exchanged our usual good mornings via text. We began to debrief the Carolina-Duke matchup the night before and I gave him the rundown on all things rushing Franklin Street before I began to clean my bathroom. We were mid-conversation when I was rushed to the hospital, unsure if we'd ever get the chance to finish it.

I wish I could've been a fly on the wall when he got the text from Kennedy that I was in the hospital with bleeding on the brain. I'm ashamed to say I still have the text thread, and even more ashamed to say I find myself rereading those messages to see if I can find the moment where things changed. He was out of town that weekend, and I later learned, he was at dinner with his family when it happened. I wonder if there was urgency on his part. I wonder if after sending the initial call to voicemail and reading that follow-up text gave him the dramatic, tinnitus-heartbeat-world spinning phenomenon that happens in the movies.

He came to visit me on one of my earlier days in the hospital, when I was very drugged and not fully awake and aware. It was so good to see him; to hear his voice, to hold his hand. I can't imagine and I won't speculate what he'd felt, considering I was half-conscious with a quarter of my head shaved. I had a tube connected to my brain, laying in a pale blue hospital gown that, again, did nothing for my skin while he spoon-fed me Chick-fil-A's chicken noodle soup. But I know for me, it was magical. My person was here, and he was gentle, caring, attentive and once again, he didn't mind playing doctor to ease my discomfort.

This wasn't necessarily the way or the time I'd want him to meet my mom, but she liked him. Things were a complete mess and okay at the same time.

The next time he visited was during week two of my hospital stay. I was in higher spirits and a better physical condition. I had graduated from physical therapy and could sit up in the chair, there was no more brain tube, and I was just a lot more Jazz, less oxycodone. It was a good day, certainly more active than the first time he visited. COVID was still high on the list of concerns, prompting him to keep his mask on during his visit. Aside from that, things almost felt normal. We laughed, we joked, we got each other up to speed on his vacation and I gave him the 4-1-1 on all things Piedmont Atlanta. We'd transitioned from playing Misery Index to setting up my laptop to catch up on the latest episode of Bel-Air since my hospital stay so rudely disrupted our weekly binge parties. I found myself needing to be held by him, even if just for a brief hug. And just like always, I melted in his arms.

Springtime is the picturesque part of the year for beautiful pastels and blooming everything, but my allergies are not quite a fan. And being holed up in a high-rise hospital room for over a week allowed me to forget the perils of pollen. All it took was an extended hug and subtle inhale of a few pollen particles from his jacket to quickly remind me that I hadn't sneezed since being admitted. As my body began to respond as it normally would to the signal from the brain of an incoming sneeze, my mind began to wonder how my head would handle it considering I hadn't made any sudden, aggressive movements since the surgery.

Uh-oh. Something doesn't feel right.

He shot me a concerned glance and a "you good?", that of which I could barely hear over the tinnitus-heartbeat-ear-ringing sensation I was beginning to experience once again. Fear and head pain welled up inside of me. I tried to shrug it off and continue watching the show but there was no ignoring this.

It's happening again.

Pressure began to build in my head and all the crippling pain I'd felt that first morning came creeping back in, this time a lot slower but just as intensely. Since he was there with me, my mom went across the street to give us privacy, grab food and give herself a break. But it was time to break some bad news to Nurse Mom again.

"I did something with that sneeze. Give me the remote to call the nurse for help and I need you to call my mom and gently tell her I need her to come back. RIGHT NOW," I said.

Within minutes, it was almost as if it was day one again and all the relief and recovery I'd made was erased.

Oh no. Did I mess something up? I just got the tube removed, will they need to put it back? Will they need to do surgery again? Oh my God, this hurts. Is this going to be my life now: A series of sneezes and back to the world of Percocet cocktails and seizure meds?

I could hear him explaining what happened to my mom as the nurse came in to essentially carry me back to the bed. I was once again in so much pain that I could do nothing but moan, cry out, and toss and turn.

The nurse began to check my vitals and left to prepare pain medicine to help calm the episode. Many agonizing minutes later, Nurse Mom was back bedside on her post and on high alert, praying and trying to calm down her wriggly daughter who was crying out in pain.

"Sit me up, sit me up."

Up the hospital bed slowly went as it inclined to be more comfortable.

"Ah! Back down, back down! It's so hot."

"Hold on, Jazmine. We're turning up the air."

I could feel their fear and concern growing as all their attempts to calm me down failed. The nurse came back in and began administering pain medicine through my IV, reassuring my mom that they'll kick in faster than if I took them orally. *Not fast enough.*

"Give me a blanket. Can you turn down the TV please? Take it off. Sit me up. It's too loud. Turn the lights off. Ouch, ouch, ouch put me back down. Oh my God, help me. It's so hot."

I continued to roll and wriggle in pain, requesting to be sat up and laid right back down for temporary bursts of relief that came with each adjusted position. Thank God I put on real bottoms before he came, because decency went out the window with that sneeze.

"Oh my God, it hurts so bad."

"Jazmine, I know it hurts but you've got to try to stay calm," my mom said. "Working yourself up isn't good for it."

Light was blinding again. My ears were ringing. The temperature was rising. The pressure made my brain feel like an expanding balloon and I was sure my head would burst open at any second. Noise was piercing. Noise—*what is that loud noise coming from outside in the hallway? PLEASE BE QUIET!*

Impeccably timed, laughter and joyful screeches taunted my ears from the group of nurses outside the room. My room was only a few feet from the nurse's desk, so I had the luxury of being a few footsteps away from help whenever needed. But at the moment, my help seemed to be having a blast while I was having a severe vasospasm episode.

They both continued to comfort me as far as they could but that was a great question. Where were my nurses, and why weren't they here trying to calm me down? The chaos in the room did not pair well with the physical unrest in my head. I just needed everyone to be quiet and still.

Nurse Mom transitioned into Momma Bear quickly, popping out into the hallway to give the nurses a warning glare and a chance to respond with a sense of urgency.

"Hey, I've gotta go meet my friend for dinner but I'm going to check on you later, okay?" he asked.

Yeah, sure, okay. I was in survival mode. I've got to get through this all over again, but at least this time, my mom was by my side, and I didn't have to do it alone. Although the pain was still present, I could tell the pain medicine began to kick in as it was becoming bearable enough to just lay still and breathe through the lingering aching. Upon calming down, I'd realized I'd wet myself somewhere during the episode and my frustrated mom once again signaled for a nurse to come tend to me.

I could hear the nurses quiet down in response to my mom's scolding.

As I lay there in my own urine listening to my mom give the nurses a good piece of her mind, I felt helpless, scared and so very weak.

Is this going to be my life now?

I was so focused on surviving so I'm glad I had my mom fighting for me, but would this be how it is now? My life at the hands and whim of whoever's responsible for taking care of me? This can't be my future. I could see my mom in and out of the room attempting to flag someone down without going too far away from me.

Not soon enough, a white nurse we weren't fond of came in to de-escalate. My mom had started to record what was happening as almost 15 minutes had passed since the first nurse provided me the medicine and no one bothered to check in or monitor what was happening with me. Shooting a glance at my mom, she hid her badge and told her she wasn't allowed to record. A heated exchange ensued, with the alleged nurse of the week more concerned with my mom's camera than the aneurysm patient actively in severe head pain.

"If you don't put your camera away, we're going to have security put you out," she threatened.

"Woah," I managed to squeeze in before my mom took back over.

"And you might as well draw up some transfer papers because if I go, she's going with me," she said.

Five feet of steel, my mom has never been afraid to speak her mind and stand up for herself. This was especially the case for her kids. I'm proud to know I get my fire from my mom. But this moment was so painful to see.

Flustered by the interaction, the nurse aggressively moved about the room.

"Find somebody else to come in here to help her. I don't want you touching her," my mom said.

One of my favorite technicians and another nurse came in and began to carefully get me and the bed cleaned and changed.

"She actually threatened to call security on you?" the tech asked in disbelief. "I am so sorry, wow."

After my bedsheets were changed, the pain slowly transitioned to that familiar heartbeat-like throb. We sat in the dark, a warm rag covered my eyes, my mouth open and my jaw riding the pulsating feeling for comfort. My mom watched in concern to ensure those movements didn't mimic that of a seizure too closely. Nurses came in frequently, asking us if we were okay and ensuring that they didn't make their mistake from earlier again.

After a bit of time passed, two Black medical personnel came in with clipboards to ask us about the incident. He introduced himself as the director of the neuro-ICU. I was still in a pretty good amount of pain, so I was hoping they'd talk quietly while I just lay there. There was still, rightfully, a bit of emotion in my mom's voice but it was infuriating how he seemed to disregard what she was saying. He turned to me to ask "my perspective" of what happened.

I sat up ever-so-slightly with the warm rag still over my eyes.

"Sir, I was in a lot of pain, and nobody was trying to help me," I began calmly but sternly. "I laid in my pee for I don't know how long. Then your nurse, who hadn't been very friendly to us since we came here, instantly threatened to call security and put out the only person who seemed to care about my pain. And now you're disregarding what she's saying and asking me like she wasn't here. My perspective is her perspective. She said what she said."

I settled back into my position and didn't say another word. They gathered their remaining information from my mom before apologizing for the incident again and leaving the room.

This was a shorter evening, as I drifted off to sleep for the day soon after. My cousin, who'd driven my mom to Atlanta, was able to come to the hospital with her since was still shaken up from the incident. I'm sure that was terrifying. And it's something especially terrifying about being present–about being there to witness it knowing there wasn't anything she could do.

I woke up feeling much better the next day than I did the night prior. I treaded carefully from then on and never saw another one of those episodes again. And neither did I see him for the rest of my time at Piedmont Atlanta.

Healing was obviously at the forefront, but I wondered when he'd be back and where he was.

Too busy. Too much to do. Too occupied. Too tired.

I'd only explicitly asked a time or two if he would come back after his last visit because I didn't want to expect too much. But that curiosity even extended to my mom, who casually asked when he'd return. I'd extended the excuses and chucked it up to be a conversation once I was released, which he met with minimal text message responses and continued absence. No call. No visit. Just sporadic texts in between "life-goes-on" while I was still processing life as I know it in the rearview.

The evening of my release, I summoned all the courage to prompt a phone call if he was free. I'd been doing good the entirety of the time we'd been getting to know each other. No stress, no pressure, no nagging. I didn't ask for much because I wanted to establish healthy boundaries and time apart. But there was no gaslighting myself out of this one. I was in the neuro-ICU for 14 days. Someone who claimed they loved and cared for me should have been there. I have difficulty opening up about being hurt by people I care about. To prepare for our conversation, I wrote my thoughts to prevent blanking on the phone. Thank God I did, because between my sweaty palms, my obnoxious heartbeat and the tremble in my throat, I don't think I would've managed to make it without my script.

"I was hoping I'd see you a little more when I was in the hospital, you know?" I began, as gently as possible, "I didn't expect you to be there every day, and I appreciated when you could come. I guess I just needed you a little more."

And my biggest irrational fear of asking for what I want and it just being too much—bordering confirmation.

"Well, I was on spring break…"

My safe, comfortable net—beginning to tear.

"I had a lot going on…"

My sure thing—not quite as certain anymore.

"But I know that's not an excuse and I won't even make them because you deserve better than that, I'm sorry," he transitioned, "I should've been up there more."

I laid in the middle of my full-size bed on top of the comforter, radio silent. I had a lump in my throat that I refused to release on the phone. I also just did not have the words.

After what I assume was too uncomfortable of a pause for him, I voiced my uncertainty on how to respond and we ended the phone call on the agreement that I needed space right now, but to know I could feel like a priority moving forward. I assumed this request—the first time during our new relationship where I placed what I felt to be a reasonable demand on him—was crystal clear. But as I reflect, I realize this was the beginning of where our love connection began to break up.

The hours of "taking it easy" at home for a busy body became agonizing. Pair that with the absence of my new, favorite person whom I typically wouldn't go hours without seeing, and I began to unravel. Two days had passed since I'd been released from the hospital, a day since our conversation. Our relationship was a safe space for open dialogue, so I thought I'd nip it in the bud to reduce the amount of mental anguish I was already facing. After muddling through a casual, delayed text conversation that dragged through the day, I dropped the bomb, so I didn't have to sleep with the distance I felt growing between us.

"Going to sleep but just in case I wasn't clear earlier, I don't want space. That was

the problem. I miss you. I needed you. I still need you."

My message was met by a 7:30 am response from him riddled with confusion: *"I thought you didn't know what you wanted from me right now."*

I responded once I woke up, before getting dressed for the day and riding back with my parents to Midtown for lunch. Along with this healed version that allowed me to exist in this love space, I was also very intentional about walking in a version that set boundaries and didn't accept less than what I need or want in the name of love. It'd been 3 days since I was discharged from the hospital after surviving a life-threatening brain injury and the man who I'd been heavily involved with had yet to show up. The message was clear, the ask seemed more than obvious: *"If not showing up then was the problem, then showing up now could've been assumed."*

I grabbed my phone mid-notification while wiping the remaining wing sauce from my fingers. All I saw was *"I care about you a lot"* and the restaurant seemed to spin. The booth we'd been comfortably seated in began to swallow me up, and there it was again. How many more times this month would I experience the dramatic, tinnitus-ears ringing sensation?

I decided it'd be best to excuse myself from the table before my dramatic reaction warranted worry from my mom. The minute I hit the stall, the tears began to fall. It was my fears. My safe, comfortable net was completely torn, leaving me free falling in stall three of the Hudson Grille bathroom. The message was long, drenched with a lot of fillers, a lot of excuses. But the point was clear, I could not and would not be a priority for him moving forward.

It didn't make sense. Although I'd allowed myself to sink into this fairytale love story we were building, I did not imagine what I felt or what we'd been doing. I'd been sitting back, passenger side, enjoying the ride because I trusted the driver for the first time in a long time. I'd believed we were heading in a great direction, having a great ride. But this was an aggressive smash on the brakes with no warning, no explanation, and a half-baked apology.

A knock on the bathroom stall jolted me out of my trance. I hadn't realized how long I'd been in the bathroom. It was a few minutes too long for Nurse Mom, who still hadn't retired from her unofficial duty.

"You alright?" She asked, "We've already paid for the food and everything."

"Oh yeah, I'm alright," I said while quickly pulling myself together behind the stall door, "I'm coming out right now."

We headed back toward my side of town while I processed the break-up text I'd just received. Perfectly timed, my parents needed to make a pit stop at the Publix around the corner to grab things for the house. With my mom's newfound love for Publix, I knew this would buy me about 20 minutes to stay back in the car and hash through the beginning of the end.

I am not crazy. I did not imagine us. He most definitely left me hanging in the hospital and he's making his escape now. And if my momma ever taught me anything, it was the ability to let somebody go when they didn't want to stay.

"*Alright, I appreciate the honesty,*" I responded, extremely hurt that such a response didn't warrant a phone call, at the very least.

He countered by thanking me for understanding and offered a phone call tonight when he'd be done for the day if I wanted to talk.

No. Actually, I don't understand. It was just "I love you" and trips to meet family, and now you're not ready? There was nothing else to talk about. As much as I hated to accept it, this is where our story ended. I cried as I swiped away from the thread, the tail end of his response ringing in my mind: "*I really did enjoy getting to know you.*"

No fight, no objections, no further protest. And just like that, I was healing from both a brain bleed and a broken heart.

I didn't understand. I could've accepted this more easily if this was where things were before the aneurysm. But things were good as gold, they were perfect.

Almost too good to be true.

I sat in the back of my Honda Accord in the Paces Ferry Publix parking lot trying not to be crushed by the weight of truth that finally reared its head. The hardest part of this heartbreak wasn't that he was leaving. It was that I couldn't understand why he was leaving *right now.*

I pondered over all the possibilities. He understood just how serious what happened to me was, so it isn't like he didn't understand. But what if he didn't? Maybe that explains why he didn't show up. Or maybe he saw how bad it was and thought I'd be like that forever and couldn't make that commitment. What would he have done if I died? I stopped toying with the assumptions swirling around my neck like a noose and decided to focus on what I could control.

I'd reflected on a joke I made to my friends when I put the finishing touches on my newly decorated room in 2021.

"Ahh, all done," I said as I did a pan of the decor in my room, "Now all I need is a lil' mans."

Quickly reneging that statement, I countered, "Actually let me make some friends first, because if a man breaks my heart before I do, I'm packing up and coming home."

I had made only three new friends at the time, one of whom was planning to leave soon. A year into my stint as an Atlanta resident and those relationships still didn't fill me the way I needed. The only one that did was just reduced to nothing but bittersweet memories.

I was just so very sure of this thing, of him, of us. I was so sure it was a God-given thing, so I was stuck asking God and myself what went wrong. I was stuck on this one, because I feel like I never truly allowed myself the grace to process and hurt from this. I was experiencing the grand duality of human emotion: Being energized and grateful that I was alive, while also mourning a relationship that was dear to me and the person I became while in it. I'd even found myself feeling guilty for feeling anything except extreme gratitude for simply being alive, while I was dying emotionally on the inside.

This chapter gives space to this experience that coincided with but was completely covered up by the aneurysm. People saw happiness. People saw the healing. But I was hurting. It's a lesson on loss and a love letter to the heartbroken girl who had to pick up the pieces and just keep moving because there were "much bigger fish to fry."

I was too busy being a miracle that I didn't allow myself to bear my brokenness.

I publicly gave God the glory but questioned the purpose in private. I smiled and rejoiced during the day and cried myself to sleep every night. I walked in my physical healing to the world and wallowed in my emotional brokenness behind closed doors. I was beginning to gain wisdom on why the old me had to go with the aneurysm, but I still couldn't wrap my head around why he had to go with her.

I wondered, what went wrong? This was bigger than a break-up, I could handle a break-up. I almost died and it seems that didn't matter to him. If the roles were reversed, I wouldn't have left his side. Because that's what you do when you almost lose someone you love: You love them harder. I felt so safe and comfortable, how do I trust myself again? It was like the rug was ripped out from under me at the very last millisecond. *How do I trust anyone else?*

Then I wandered over to start asking these questions of The One who has all the answers. Does God change His mind? God knows us. He knows the future. He knows what will happen before we do. He knows our hearts and what we are capable of, so I wondered why in the world did God put him in my life knowing he wouldn't have the heart to stay? God is intentional, what is the lesson I was supposed to learn from this? How do we translate the things we felt were God-given at first, which God then took away?

And as I began to acknowledge that this pain was big enough to take to God, he acknowledged my cries and gave me an answer. It was intentionally placed before the first word that gave me peace about my aneurysm. It came after months of heavy spiritual warfare I'd later experience.

I was sitting in disbelief. I just so happened to be invited to this pop-up service by a new friend. It was hosted by a church and pastor I'd never heard of. Yet, I started hearing answers to everything I'd been questioning in frustration for the past two months.

"How long will you mourn over that which I've rejected?" Dr. Dharius Daniels referenced God's conversation with Samuel about Saul in 1 Samuel 16.

I repositioned in my seat, instantly feeling spoken to.

"I'm done with it. Even though you're crying over it, I'm done with it. And even though you still love Saul, I'm done with it. And even though you wish it wasn't going to be this way, I'm done with it. And even if it doesn't make sense, I'm done with it," he continued. This message was at the top of his pop-up Atlanta service's message, titled, "I Don't Need Closure."

"God orchestrates endings. And I think there's an ending He wants to orchestrate in most of us watching, listening to this message. I don't believe He would put this message on my heart if this were not an ending, He wants to orchestrate in yours. I believe He put this message in my heart because there's something He wants to bring to an end in yours. Because it's keeping some of us stuck... and there needs to be an ending to our need for explanations."

I was floored. The tears began to flow. My experience helped me realize more often when I was hearing from God. But I was overwhelmed with how God was speaking to me and my situation right then. Everything I questioned, literally the exact way I questioned God, was being answered in the warm-up section of this Pastor's sermon. I received it as a message to me about the loss of that relationship, but also a beautifully painful symbol that not all that is lost are losses. God sometimes orchestrates endings that aren't endings at all, but paths into greener pastures.

I'd been so frustrated at God because I wondered why He'd give me something I prayed for just to take it away. Then I realized, it was still what I prayed for. I asked God to show me I was worthy of receiving the love I desired, and He did. But I also asked God to teach me how to let go of things when they no longer were good for me, and He did. Sometimes we learn the best lessons from God in ways that may seem contradictory. But how else will we learn what we can handle without being tested to show if we can handle it? How will you see if your heart is still soft if God doesn't throw you any hardballs? How will you ever know if you're ready for the things you're praying for, if you don't receive things that aren't ready for you?

I couldn't understand the timing and why it had to happen in this season. I honestly still catch myself praying for a cause and closure. But I began to come to terms with the fact that maybe that was just the purpose. This season taught me that everything won't come labeled with a reason. I still don't understand, but that's okay. The call was to learn to trust God even when you can't see the why.

I occasionally find myself wrestling with feelings that resurface since I denied myself the chance to mourn the loss of that relationship then. I occasionally scroll through old messages, hoping new revelation would reveal itself within blue blocks of iMessage. I'll occasionally flip through the pages of *Seven Days in June*, longing for the days of the new book smell and reflecting on my very own seven weeks in spring.

For everything, there is a season. And my seven weeks in spring were meant to be just that.

8

Carry Me Home

"God, I don't know what part of the plan this is, or what chapter this gon' be, but I know it's gon be one heck of a story..."

I opened my apartment door, unsure how I felt or how to respond. A bittersweetness filled my mouth as the familiar tropical fragrance filled my nostrils. My stomach did a slight lurch, and my heart felt as if it was fluttering in my chest as I stepped through the door of the place just two weeks ago, I'd experienced so much physical pain. I thought I'd be relieved and happy to be home, but all I felt was triggered.

Walking around the oversized island, I thought back to Kennedy rushing to get water as I collapsed to the hardwood floors a few steps away. Stepping into the living room, I felt the lights peeking through the open blinds and remembered the piercing pain as the morning sun became a hazard as the headache intensified. I eased each Nike Air Max off with the opposite foot and sank into our sectional, thinking back to the frightening convulsion my body made after attempting to lay down mid-hemorrhage. Here I was, back in the place I'd been wishing I could be for the past two weeks, and all I could think about was the fear and pain I now associated with it.

Triggers aside, having my backside resting in a quality, comfortable seat felt amazing, unlike the medical hospital bed and chair I'd grown accustomed to. I sat momentarily, trying to process the myriad of emotions I was feeling. Relief and fear, comfort and worry, freedom and uncertainty all at once. The only thing I was sure of was that I had to use the bathroom, and for the first time in two weeks, I didn't have to report it to anyone, and I didn't need any help doing so.

"Where you going, you need help?" my mom asked as I got up from the couch.

Almost didn't have to report it.

"To the bathroom, Ma," I said, "Remember, I'm not in the hospital anymore."

"Okay, but just don't overdo it."

And I didn't plan to, but the minute I walked into my bedroom, "overdo it" became an understatement. My bathroom was only accessible by entering my bedroom, which I did not find how I left it. Between the family members who'd driven my mom to Atlanta and stayed the first week, and her and my stepdad, my usually carefully arranged bedroom was in disarray and stressed me out. After digesting the clutter in my room, I remembered I had to use the bathroom and took the sharp left to step into it, which also did not look how I left it. I was in the middle of cleaning when the aneurysm ruptured, so someone cleared and cleaned the Fabuloso & Ajax concoctions left marinating in the sink, toilet and tub. But the perfectionist in me was perturbed that I did not return to a perfectly undisturbed home.

Against Nurse Mom's directions, I'd begun arranging and organizing things to my liking, a masked attempt at trying to maintain some semblance of control after being so restricted and surrendered for the past 14 days. The shuffling warranted a peep-in from my mom, who attempted to help as much as possible to prevent me from overwhelming myself. I transitioned from the bathroom to my closet–which was already not enough space for my large wardrobe–and began adjusting, compacting and removing their things. My mom was also trying to help organize their bags and clothes but any time she moved something, I moved it elsewhere. In frustration, she gave up and let me handle the rearranging task that I was attacking like a madwoman.

After collecting their belongings and neatly condensing to a section in my room, I finally felt I could rest. I sank into the middle of our plush sectional, facing the cushions as tears began to form in the corner of my eyes. My mom was unhappy with the inappropriate amount of physical activity I'd just completed and reading the room, she and Gerald went to the store to give me some space.

I thought I'd be overjoyed to be home. Truthfully, I realized I was just happy to be out of the hospital, and even that was disgruntling. I experienced this big high, only to be met with crushing triggers when I walked through the door, which brought me crashing down. Physically, I was much more comfortable in my own space but mentally, I couldn't pinpoint why I felt so low. I was exhausted, confused, triggered, annoyed, frustrated and slightly afraid. It was almost like I wanted to be back in the hospital, surrounded by the comfort of an on-call nurse and familiarity with a low-maintenance routine. With the space I so desperately needed to just experience the emotions I was feeling, I laid there and cried myself into a midday nap.

I woke up to my mom and Gerald returning to the apartment, having taken another trip to Publix and coming home with goodies. I was in a much better mood–you aren't you when you're sleepy–but I could still feel a layer of heaviness under the surface that I was sure I'd eventually have to come to terms with. It was all new, and I just needed time to process it. I almost died. I was back in the space where it happened. I was hospitalized for two weeks. I was physically recovering from bed rest and on top of this miraculous experience, I was having boy trouble. *Fun.*

After realizing my frustration was from a heightened sense of lack of control, I decided to take it easier on Nurse Mom and to take it easy overall. I didn't roll my eyes when I heard the frequent, "take it easy." I didn't object when she'd snatch the milk jug or juice carton from my hands, although we were well past my 24-hour warning. I didn't complain when she deemed me too fragile and took on all the cooking and cleaning. I rode the wave of post-hospital recovery, and soaked up all the perks that came with it. I postponed reciting the spoken word piece I'd planned to do on social media live for another day. Instead, for the rest of day one, I relaxed on our cloud of a sectional and watched TV without a care in the world, manning the calls from loved ones as they came in.

I realized I could finally shower, and I was overjoyed. This warranted worry from my momma, who insisted an unsupervised shower was too dangerous. Since I'd exchanged my protests for peace, we compromised on a bubble bath, but she wasn't budging on the supervision. I figured I'd given up privacy and control the past 14 days, what harm would one more day do? I sat in the tub of warm water, knees to chest, and hair scattered all over my head feeling like a kid again as my mom poured water down my back to rinse off the soap. Never in a million years would I imagine being back in this position as a grown woman. I'm sure there's a picture I mentally recalled, or my brain is searching for fragmented pieces of a childhood memory, but I see this exact moment 20 or so years ago.

We are in Ahoskie and I'm in the bathtub of my childhood home, my momma crouched over the side scrubbing me with a kiddie bubble bath formula. Scrubbing off the outside I'd brought in but praying and washing away the impurities of the outside world off her youngest girl. We were reenacting that scene 20 years later, except I'm 23 years old and in my Atlanta mid-rise. This time she's attempting to scrub off sticky medical tape residue, praying and washing away the 14 days of hospital that was layered on me so thickly.

Instead of shame or pride, I felt this overwhelming sense of safety. I felt like a little girl again, with nothing to fear because momma was right there. In a feeling I couldn't grasp in such an intimate moment, I now realize this was love. This was the opposite of that nagging feeling of being so far away from home that I'd been experiencing. I'd always been a momma's girl, but this reminded me of how good it feels to be sheltered, covered and protected if I just surrendered. Earlier in my frustration, I considered kicking her out and here I was wondering what I would have done without her–what I'd ever do without her. She dropped everything to be there with me and it was no different now that I was back home. She planned to be with me until I was better. I remembered my revelation in the hospital and moved forward accepting the help.

After my bath, I showed my mom and stepdad how to open the pullout couch. I gave them fresh sheets and returned to my room. Kennedy had recently come in from work and prepped for bed herself. She knocked on my door and made her way in. She sat on the corner of my bed as we caught up on boy drama, work happenings and roommate conversation we'd missed from the past two weeks.

"Kennedy, you saved my life. Thank you," I said.

"Girl, bye! Don't start this mushy stuff with me," she giggled.

I laughed with her but repeated my sentiments so she knew I was grateful to her. We'd obviously grown to know each other well by living together for the past eight months. But it was very touching that she not only took me to the hospital, but stayed with me until surgery, came back after and visited me in the second week of my stay. I knew that it could only be God that she had even been home that morning, and I later learned from her of just how impactful my experience and recovery was for her mental health too.

As much as I looked forward to a great first night of rest in my bed, I was awakened not long after midnight by commotion outside and could not go back to sleep for hours. My body was still on round-the-clock meds and hospital time, so I prayed and talked to God, cried a bit, scrolled on socials, and watched a bit of *My Wife and Kids* until I eventually fell asleep hours later.

A few days of this in combination with Kennedy's late work schedule; my feeling bad that my parents were sleeping on the couch; and talking through arrangements for how to get my mom back home and I was torn between letting my help go home a little earlier than I expected or returning to Ahoskie with them for a couple of weeks. Gerald had to return home a week after my discharge, which was a week before my driving restriction would be lifted, and even with momma still here with me, we'd be stuck in the house if it meant her getting behind the wheel and on Metro Atlanta's busy roads. But if I went home, I'd be eight hours away from my doctors and the hospital in case of an emergency. I was cleared by the doctors and hadn't experienced any medical issues. I even cleared my primary care physician's check-in. But I was still so overcome with fear with being away from the people that saved me–that could save me if something else went wrong.

And then it hit me.

When did you put your faith in the doctors instead of God?

I realized that a lot of my fear when I was first released from the hospital came from being out of call-button distance away from medical staff who could tend to me quickly if needed. But a few days removed from their care, I felt less dependent on round-the-clock supervision. But now I was floating the idea of being hours away. I was lucky then, but what do my chances look like when Piedmont Atlanta isn't a quick drive up the road, but rather a helicopter transport to the nearest hospital with a neuro team?

This wasn't walking in faith.

Luck had nothing to do with it, it never did. I was blessed; intentionally covered by the blood no matter if I was an eight minute or eight-hour drive away. If I was going to die, then it would've worked out that I died the moment I experienced a rare phenomenon that Mayo Clinic and the National Institutes of Health cites less than 200,000 people experience a year; one which carries a higher morbidity and mortality rate than any other form of stroke.

Faith can be described as belief or trust in something for which there isn't direct proof. But as a newly coined "walking testimony," my new name was synonymous with the phrase "living proof." I was reminded that if faith was an issue true to its definition, I was all the proof I needed. My life, my condition, the fact that I was approaching a week post-discharge, and I hadn't experienced a single headache. I could talk, walk, think like I used to, a luxury—a blessing—that 66.667% of SAH survivors do not have. So how dare I sit there and contemplate just how far away was safe when the God that saved me then is the same God who is near and far off? Standing on the promises of my Jehovah-Rapha, I packed my bag and took the long drive home to surprise my relatives, who were only expecting the return of my mom and stepdad.

I shared the backseat of Gerald's bright red Chevrolet Silverado—affection-ately nicknamed 'Big Red'—with Cinnamon. She was formerly my sister's sweet Maltipoo, but now my new emotional support pup. I'd spent most of the ride sleeping, eating or on my phone, with an early pit stop at a gas station to buy me a neck pillow after my mom insisted I needed something to support my head. The last time I'd taken the eight-hour drive was New Year's Eve after losing my previous puppy-in-crime to a vicious pit bull attack. Here, I vowed I was never making the drive again. But the eight hours isn't so bad when you're not in the driver's seat or making the ride home with an empty passenger seat and a car full of heartbreak. Before I knew it, we were exchanging the four-lane interstate for narrow, two-way highway roads; my favorite indicator that we were almost home. As we crossed the bridge on South Academy street in Ahoskie, I began to be oddly overcome with emotion.

"Oh look, we're home. Hey Ahoskie! Oh my gosh I think I'm going to cry," I said between nervous giggles.

My mom and Gerald weren't paying much attention to me, but I noticed my mom slightly shaking her head and smirking in response to my comment. She soon did a double take as she quickly looked back and caught me crying.

"You're crying?!" she asked in confusion.

"She's crying?!" Gerald also chimed in.

"YES, I SAID I WAS GOING TO CRY," I said between tears, still nervously laughing.

I couldn't articulate how I was suddenly so overcome with emotion. It was a feeling I didn't know I'd have to grow very familiar with in the coming months. But crossing the bridge on South Academy and seeing the Creek Amphitheater in the distance on the left where I'd spent many teenage days or seeing the lush green trees after passing the repair shop where I'd gotten my first car repaired after my first accident, the memories flooded in, and it all felt like my life was flashing before my eyes. I rarely saw this place again, and a part of me felt like I would never return. My soul was so happy, the happiest it'd ever been to be back home in little ol' Ahoskie.

As we pulled into our neighborhood, we drove past all three of my sisters taking a stroll with my cousins around the neighborhood. My mom had called letting them know we'd be arriving shortly, but they didn't know I was with them. So, when Gerald pulled Big Red up beside them and slowly rolled the backseat window down, they were pleasantly surprised to see me peek my head out.

"Hey sisters!" I said as I opened the door to get out.

Without a doubt, I am the emotional one in the family, so hugging among us wasn't common. But this moment warranted one. I jumped down from Big Red and grabbed the first one I could get my hands on. Once again, emotion flooded in, and I cried. Similarly to never seeing Ahoskie again, there was almost a moment where I thought I'd never see my sisters again. While it was some pretty scary stuff experiencing a traumatic brain bleed in real time, the scariest part about it was leaving my family behind. Of course, they poked fun at me for walking in my family nickname as the "Bucket of Water," but that was fine. I just needed to show them that I loved them and was happy to still be here with them, a luxury our brother, Travis could no longer indulge in. I decided to stay outside and walk with them as mom and Gerald went to the house with my bags. My mom bid an ordinal "take it easy" as Gerald pulled off, and I'm certain she watched me until I was out of eyeshot as they drove away. We walked and talked. They asked me specific questions about my experience and told me what it was like to be on the other end of the phone call that day. After a lap and a half, I bowed out as we passed our place, so I didn't overwhelm myself. My mom came and sat outside, and we'd catch the attention of everyone who knew us that rode by the house.

"Is that Jazmine!?"
    "It's good to see you're home, girl!"
    "Look at God! We've been praying for you."

Family and friends who knew I was in town wanted to "lay eyes on me," while others couldn't believe their eyes when they did. It felt like the days in the New Testament when believers and unbelievers would gather to witness firsthand the amazing, unbelievable things the disciples were spreading throughout the land. I took this experience to walk proudly in being both a first-hand witness and walking evidence of God's goodness, and I never failed to give him the credit for it. My favorite moment that reminded me just how miraculous of a recovery I had was an interaction one day at the local Dollar General. My mom and I walked into the store, and I was trailing just a few feet behind her when my old first-grade teacher walked by.

"Hey Trina, how's your baby doing?" she asked.

"She's right here, ask her," my mom said as she motioned to me.

Even with the mask, her facial expression could've been the textbook example of someone who looked as if they've seen a ghost. She was speechless. She voiced a muffled "oh my God" as I amusingly responded, "isn't He good?"

* * *

I spent the days at home resting, recovering and simply relaxing. I was on paid short-term disability leave at work, and I was settling into the routine of just simply existing. Being back home surrounded by love felt so good, especially because this allowed me to run from the soft breakup I had just experienced. I went to the kids' baseball games, attended my hometown church—where I was affectionately received and invited to share my testimony–I lounged around with Cinnamon, and spent time with the family and friends I'd been so far away from.

There were scares; from neck cramps from new pillows and improper sleeping positions that kept me on the nurse's hotline. But it was nothing that Tylenol and prayer couldn't fix. There were moments at the kids' baseball games where I'd get carried away with screaming and experience a pressure shift in my head that reminded me that although my recovery was miraculous, it was still active. I had moments where I couldn't quite keep up with everyone, so while they were outside on the porch chatting, I'd be in the quiet house recharging with a nap. I was balancing taking advantage of my freedom and not overdoing it. The only physical evidence of my aneurysm was the quickly regrowing patch of hair in the front that I'd creatively learned to style around. I was truly a walking miracle, walking faithfully in my healing and enjoying my recovery. I proved to everyone who knew my story that God is still in the business of miracles, signs and wonders.

But one day, I realized I hadn't fully understood what that meant.

I made lunch plans with Ms. Barbara, my special family friend who'd known me literally before I was born. The clock read one p.m., and her white Chevrolet Cruze was parked out front to pick me up for our lunch at Tavern 125. We talked on the 15-minute drive to Murfreesboro, the neighboring town just a short drive over, where we carried our conversation into the restaurant. We texted and FaceTimed often, but we'd always catch up over lunch when I was in town. We talked, ate, and laughed, and as we shared a spinach dip appetizer that I learned was her recipe, I realized our lunch was just another reminder of how often we take life and our loved ones for granted.

"I was so worried about you," she said, "I called your mom every single day. I cried so much."

We'd both shot the waitress a quick thank you as she placed our meals in front of us. I remembered her calls, specifically a worried face on the FaceTime screen when I was too weak to handle calls myself. But I was genuinely surprised that she said she was so emotionally distressed.

"Really? You were? Why were you crying so much?" I asked.

"What do you mean? I was worried sick, although I'd talk to your mom often, I just never knew what could happen."

The unexpected look of bewilderment on my face prompted her next question.

103

"Jazmine, do you realize the odds?" she asked.

The hot, fried seafood platter before me that was mouthwatering just a minute ago became instantly unappetizing. Her voice felt further and further away as I seemed to shrink inside myself while she casually explained the mortality and recovery rate for people who suffer from brain aneurysms.

I didn't realize the odds. Or the statistics. Or the numbers. I didn't even think about them. I was present in my experience, but I was so steeped in my faith and healing that it was never a shadow of a doubt in that hospital that I was going to recover. I woke up after surgery and I was still me, all me, and I didn't feel at all physically different from the person who I was before they put me under. That inexplicable physical recovery, the fact that once the initial emergency was over and all I had to deal with were some pesky migraines, led me not to believe anything other than what God and my faith was telling me: that I was going to live.

But it really could have been so different.

I don't think it hit me until then how very scary what happened to me was. How close to death I was—how close to death I still could be. All the fear, all the worry, all the unbelief and doubt that I simply did not even think to have in the hospital flooded over me. This was further proof that had I walked in fear instead of faith, it would have handicapped my healing, because here I was crippled by worry of something that had already happened, stressing over something that God already had control of. We wrapped up our lunch and I took most of my meal to go as my appetite never returned. When I got home, I probed my mom for answers I knew she didn't have, not realizing I was actually looking for a supernatural peace.

"I really could've died."

"Were you worried I was going to die?"

"Did you know survival statistics for aneurysms?"

"People go into comas or become blind," I fired off each without waiting for a response to the previous.

My thoughts were racing, my heart was pounding, and I teared up as the realization flooded over me.

I almost died.

I can't explain how this never fully dawned on me. It'd been two weeks since being released from the hospital and I was doing well. In the beginning, as with any emergency, I thought about the possibility of death. But I'd gotten to the point where I was so at peace with God's Will, that it never really crossed my mind again. I took my experience and condition very seriously. Still, I was so settled into the miraculous evidence of my condition that there was truly no room for anything other than life-giving thoughts. I, once again, focused my thoughts on that. If I could have peace then, at the height of uncertainty, why let fear rule my thoughts? If my Father, who has the world in His hands, told me that I would live and constantly did the work to prove it, who was I to go against His word? Especially when It's done nothing but kept and comforted me for the past month.

"Jazmine, you just gotta keep that same faith," she said.

With my mom giving external validation of exactly what I was thinking, I wiped my tears, took a deep breath and chose to walk in faith rather than fear. I allowed those statistics, those scary numbers and those worrisome probabilities to fuel my faith. Many people who experience the aneurysm I had don't make it out alive, but I did. A good portion of people have lasting ailments, but I don't. A large percentage of survivors can't go back to life as normal following their condition or treatment, but I can. And for that, instead of succumbing to fear like the enemy intended, I was energized and back at peace.

* * *

Springtime in Ahoskie was ending, and I dreaded returning to all I ran away from in Atlanta. I thought about all the things waiting on me: Being homesick again, but now, also dealing with heartbreak from the loss of the one thing that made it feel more like home. There was also the loneliness, being away from family and my return to work was approaching sooner as the May days flew by.

I still struggle with giving myself grace for returning to work so soon. I was physically okay, and I walked in the belief that I should be glad I was blessed enough to do so. So as the countdown began to go back to work in June, I planned my return to Atlanta for the end of May with enough time to settle into being back in my own space and alone before having to resume life as normal.

Between doing nothing all day and the comfort of being surrounded at every moment by people I knew and loved, I struggled to convince myself that I was still supposed to be in Atlanta on my own. I was on a casual Facetime call with Gwen when this feeling was unintentionally teased. We discussed my impending return to Georgia and one of her jokes paired too well with my intrusive thoughts.

"Jazmine, nothing good has come from you moving to Atlanta. You should just come back home," she joked.

I laughed with her, but part of me seriously considered how this random quip was exactly what was in my subconscious. I hadn't shared it with anyone. For the second time, I experienced a traumatic incident that brought me back home for an extended period. The first was having to witness my one-year-old Maltipoo be mauled by a pit bull, which led me to spend the entire month of December in Ahoskie in 2021. Now, here was the worst-case scenario turned real, where I had a life-threatening condition that was a coin toss away from never seeing my family again. Instead of voicing these worries with her, I thought of how God shepherded me back to peace after my bout of extreme anxiety. I decided this could be a moment of spiritual growth. I didn't speak on it any further, and soon after ending our call, I immediately retreated to my bedroom for prayer.

I was still very new to this level of relationship with God. It was one thing to call on Him in an emergency or in desperate need of saving. But if He could answer my prayers then, He could give me guidance and wisdom for the everyday decisions I'd previously thought I made on my own. I still believed that Atlanta was divinely enabled, so it only made sense to consult the Giver of the gift in the first place. I'd gotten into a heel sitting position on the floor in front of my bedroom window, facing the sunshine beaming through the blinds.

Okay God, I feel like Atlanta was all you. It could've only been you. And after all that's happened and all the things that have brought me back home, I'm starting to wonder if maybe Atlanta isn't where I'm supposed to be anymore. I don't know, that's why I'm here. So, I will try this thing where I come to you for answers. Not my mom. Not my friends. But I need to know from YOU if I'm supposed to go back to Atlanta or if this is a sign that I'm supposed to be here. And I'll wait for you, whether you tell me now or later. For the rest of the day, I'll be listening for you.

I made a practice of sitting for a few minutes after my devotional for a response from God. Prayer is a conversation, after all. But once my timer went off, I made a final nod to let Him know that I was still listening, however He decided to let me know. I went on about my day, not knowing exactly when or how I'd hear from God, and truthfully, not sure if that was how it even worked.

As the day went on, my mom told me someone wanted to see me. This wasn't uncommon. My time at home was filled with friends, family and not-so-familiar folks who just wanted to "lay eyes on me." But as my mom described how the woman knew us, it was difficult to confidently say I remembered her. I chalked it up to her being one of the not-so-familiar folks from my childhood that I might recognize once I saw her, and we swung by the store where she worked as a cashier while we were out getting lunch. Seeing her didn't jog any memories for me, so I went in politely but very indifferently. Little did I know, this random conversation was about to be the answer to my prayers.

Her name was Sonya. She'd asked me if I remembered her, to which I gave an honest no, and she recalled a recent conversation with my aunt.

"Your aunt told me that you mentioned you were scared of planes?" she questioned as the confused look on my face caused her to elaborate, "Or she said you might've been scared to go back to Atlanta?"

I was a bit confused. I knew the fear of planes was true years ago, but I'm a frequent flier now. And although I'd seen my aunt the day I'd gotten to Ahoskie, I don't recall voicing any fear, especially not my subconscious fear of returning to Atlanta. So, my spirit-man perked up after realizing what was happening before my mind could rationalize my way out of it. She told me how she'd been keeping up with my progress on Facebook from my sister and loved the spoken word piece I made about my experience.

"Get on that plane and go home,"

My jaw fell to the floor.

"Remember what you said in that poem, don't be scared. Keep that same faith you had in the hospital," she said, before finishing with a firm, "Go back to Atlanta, girl."

I was flabbergasted. It was so quick that I almost couldn't believe it. So direct that I was slightly terrified. I was standing there in disbelief that God sat so very high on His throne yet looked to the lowliest of low places–4.31 square miles in all its glory–and put it on the heart of a cashier at Duck Thru #31 in Ahoskie, North Carolina to give me the exact answer I'd been praying for. Not only did He give me the guidance I was seeking, but He did it in such a blatant way that it couldn't be denied that it could only be Him.

I could only utter small 'wows' as she continued to pull pieces from my poem. They were pieces that I based on the Word and didn't even realize. That was another very subtle confirmation that God was speaking then, because it was so unintentionally steeped in His Word, which can't come back to Him void. I was much more heedful leaving the store than I was coming in, and once we got back into the car, I had to explain to my mom just how powerful what just happened was.

I'd just sat in prayer that very morning begging for God to give me answers. I didn't consult a soul, because I wanted to know and I needed to see what exactly I was supposed to do next, but only from God Himself. A part of me thought it'd come mysteriously, like in a fortune cookie or through a random song lyric on the radio. But He used a stranger to give me direct orders on what I was supposed to do. Underneath this semi-stranger's raspy, feminine voice, I heard the whisper of a familiar Voice.

Get back on that plane and go home. Keep that same faith.

Simple, yet comforting. It was a reminder of how the same way His power and strength were made perfect in my weakness before, it can and will be done again; over and over, for the rest of my life if I just allow Him to do so. I had faith in Him to save my life, surely, I could trust Him to guide me on how to best live it. I confirmed my arrangements back to Atlanta on the car ride home, not exactly sure of all the steps, but knowing my God would order them. It was more than bittersweet to leave my family after such a scary incident and a comfortable few weeks. But I knew that I couldn't stay in Ahoskie forever. Something was waiting for me in Atlanta. I wrapped up my last few days in my hometown, put on my big girl pants and mentally prepared myself to resume my Atlanta storyline.

* * *

I made a pit stop in Raleigh where I usually fly back to Atlanta from RDU. Before returning home, I hitched a ride with Gwen to Charlotte, North Carolina for our friend, Taleah's graduation party. A prolonged, tearful hug met me. I almost forgot this was the first time she'd seen me since the aneurysm. Taleah was a nursing school graduate, so she had a technical idea of what I'd experienced, which probably made our reunion even more bittersweet. In another moment of overwhelming emotion, a weekend spent with some of my closest friends was exactly what I needed before flying back. Gwen and I returned to the Triangle the next day, and I made my way to the airport after another tearful departure.

After passing through security and boarding, I settled into the window seat of the Frontier airplane. I took deep breaths underneath my mask. It was May 16th. A day shy of a full month ago, I was released from the hospital after a subarachnoid hemorrhage. Today, I was returning to Atlanta to be on my own again, soon to return to work. I honestly don't know what was crazier... that I was alive, my healing and recovery, or that I was going back to work full-time just two months after a near-death experience. Physically, I felt normal. I was walking in gratitude and fully embracing the miracle. If I was blessed enough to be able to return to work, why not do so?

Once boarding completed, I opened my window shade and watched as the plane taxied the runway. Although I'd become a frequent flier and tossed my fear of flying to the wind sophomore year of college, I still wasn't the biggest fan of being tens of thousands of feet in the air. To combat that anxiety, I was the flier who went to sleep the minute the plane was in the air. If I woke up, I didn't mind sneaking a peek or a picture of the skies, but I would close the window and my eyes and brace myself for landing and takeoff. I didn't want to see it. I think it was still a valid level of fear associated with being so out of control and at the mercy of someone else that would rightfully terrify anyone. But I just experienced the scariest freefall of faith, and the Creator of the skies kept me from hitting the ground. How could I ever fear gliding through those same skies governed by the same God ever again? So, with this ride, I watched the plane take off. I sat in fascination as, for the first time, I watched as everything slowly transitioned to tiny specks of land below as we ascended further into the sky. Amazed, I watched the moment we transitioned through and above the clouds. I was overwhelmed with the beauty and I was at peace with being at the mercy of God in all aspects.

I'd been missing out on so much just on the other side of that plane shade.

My motto during my recovery came from a Warner Bros "for your consideration" panel I cut at work from a talkback of the film, "King Richard." In the conversation, Will Smith said, "fear and doubt are the opposite of faith and God," a quote I've since lived by and allowed to breathe life in me in the hospital. But another powerful antidote from Smith was in an interview where he dropped the gem, "the best things in life are on the opposite side of fear." This moment was the exact personification of just that. I'd been hopping on planes, praying for safe travels and missing out on the magnificent views because evidently, I didn't fully trust the prayer or the pilot. What a life half-lived.

What a life half-lived.

What a metaphor. I realized I'd been living my life just like that. On the journey but not fully trusting the Divine Pilot because I was failing to be present for the ride. Or I was afraid to open the window and take in the breath-taking views. I reflected on how unhappy and unsatisfied I was before the aneurysm. I reflected on how stuck I felt, so seized by fear to do the things I once dreamed of doing. I was struggling with being in a new city post-graduation and mid-pandemic. Imposter syndrome and post-graduate depression were running amuck, and I was in a job that I was grateful for, but not content with. This experience felt like a radical turning point. It was a chance to see that life is too short not to do what I want, like popping open the shade and seeing life above the clouds, especially because of something as trivial as fear. I stared out the window in deep reflection and devotion the entire hour and a half flight. Once we landed, the pilot's voice snapped me out of my unintentional meditation.

"Ladies and gentleman, welcome to Hartsfield Jackson International in Atlanta, Georgia."

God carried me home. Out of the hospital and back to my place. Out of Atlanta and back to my hometown. And now, back from Ahoskie to this place I was still trying to figure out how exactly to make feel like home. This time, I had divine assurance that I wouldn't be figuring it out alone.

Home, bittersweet home, Atlanta.

9

Take Me to the Water

"Because if the devil was gonna wage war on me like he was trying to, I knew I was gonna need armor like no other, to make it through to tell this story like no other."

I once again stood in front of my apartment. This time, my only companions were my returned copy of *Seven Days in June* at the foot of the door, and the impending heartbreak waiting to be dealt with as soon as I stepped inside.

I was greeted by the familiar tropical aromas that floated in the air as I walked in. A lot less triggered than the first time, I was grateful that I didn't have to take that physical first step alone into the place where I thought I'd die. But I knew taking *this* step alone would be the first step mentally toward my healing.

There were so many devils to face being back in the space where I almost lost my life. There was the trigger of being in a place that's supposed to breed comfort, taunting me with its emptiness from my previous relationship. There was overcoming the fear of physically being alone. I was still reckoning with the loss of my brother and emotional support pup, which

113

were heightened by my own close encounter with death—the biggest devil to wrestle with. And to top the trauma cake, I was going to have to reckon with it physically, all by myself. I knew that God was with me on this journey, but I prioritized praying for physical manifestations of Him in Atlanta to help me on my way. Until then, I heavily relied on my village who kept me encouraged virtually.

From the increased frequency of FaceTime calls from mom to group calls with my best friends and other good friends, I didn't spend much time alone, truly preparing for the return to work as I expected. I'd wake up, have my morning devotional, lounge around and rest while still on the phone with someone or a series of people for most of the day. Then I'd wind down and have prayer time before bed.

Though I was still adjusting to everything, I felt I was still in a solid place after all that had happened. Physically, I felt great. I made the life-or-death ordeal in the hospital look like an easy feat. But the mental warfare to follow was an entirely different beast I wasn't prepared for.

We've all reckoned with our personal relationship to death. Being so far away. Being scared when it's your time. But I was brave. I was at peace. I surrendered. I thought about my brother and how I could tell him everything I'd been speaking to a gravestone for the past three years. My return to work was scheduled for June 1st, a day after the anniversary of his passing. I was able to take his birthday and anniversary dates as a bereavement day with my job, so it was sad to be back in Atlanta alone grieving his passing without family for the first time after such a close encounter myself. With that sitting at the surface and nothing but time on my hands to reckon with it, I felt a lot heavier. I attempted to mask it, hoping I could pray it away and focus on how good God was for saving my life, so nothing else should matter. The week before my return, my manager asked if I wanted to work from home until I felt up to returning in person.

"I think I'll come in. Being around people might do me some good," I told her.

Anything to get back to normal.

On the morning of my scheduled return, I ran into a hurdle I almost completely forgot about since I hadn't been leaving the house the past few weeks: my hair. Kudos to myself, I packed my lunch and picked my outfit the night before: one of my meal prep combos I had plenty of time to make. For the outfit, I chose my favorite light-colored plaid pants and a burgundy "sis, you good?" Target graphic tee. But when I stepped in front of the mirror to do my hair, I realized I hadn't considered that I was still working with a fist-sized (but growing) bald spot and unable to use any product as it healed. I struggled with several combinations, becoming increasingly frustrated as each was a failure. Then my overactive tear ducts began to do what they do best. Every black girl knows the pain of fighting with a failed twist out when you've got places to be. Imagine that frustration as a rug over a nasty, festering hole in the carpet you'd been attempting to cover for weeks. After my final attempt to incorporate a scarf just wasn't doing it for me, I lost it. I sobbed uncontrollably, my face was a bright red and my head began to hurt from all the pulling and manipulation.

But this was not a regular cry.

My heart was racing. My breathing was in uncontrollable, shallow breaths and my hands shook intensely. I sat on the closed toilet to try to calm myself down. I knew I was frustrated but I didn't intend to work myself up this much. It seemed to be getting more out of control by the second.

Oh my gosh, I'm having a panic attack.

I called Gwen, whose excitement upon answering was quickly replaced with concern when she realized this was a 9-1-1 call.

"Breathe. Breathe," she said.

I only knew what was happening because I experienced it once before. It was when I first returned to my Chapel Hill apartment to start the school year after losing Travis in 2020. I was sitting in my bedroom, and one of those unexpected reminders that you'll never see that person again fell over me so heavily. Thankfully, I could breathe through it, but I'd never experienced another emotion so intensely, nor did I have an episode since. Until this morning, when my stupid hair didn't want to stay in its stupid place for me to return to my stupid job after having a stupid aneurysm.

And it clicked. It wasn't just about my hair. *I wasn't ready.*

I wasn't ready to fix my hair in the mornings before work. I wasn't ready to return to work. I wasn't ready to return to normal.

An abnormal thing happened to me just two months ago. For whatever reason, I put on this big smile, thanked God and put a timeclock on my healing, forcing my mind and my emotions to keep up with my physical condition. That is not how it works. I'd been riding this wave of extreme gratitude that I didn't realize nestled underneath it, was a hidden layer of toxic positivity. I didn't fully process the extent of how scary what happened to me was because I was hyper-focused on the miracle. I didn't allow myself to truly heal from the heartbreak of losing an important relationship because I could've lost my life. I thought I ought to be grateful instead. I didn't let myself acknowledge the fear that constantly gnawed at me that something else bad would happen because 'fear is the opposite of faith' and I didn't subscribe to fear anymore.

But with anything, continued pressure can only lead to an explosion. The final incendiary was the failed attempt to whip my hair into shape for my all-too-soon return to work. As I calmed down and explained to Gwen what was happening, it all came pouring out.

I was scared. As I struggled to grasp the words to explain this lurking sense of fear, she finished my sentence, perfectly encapsulating what I'd been terrified to admit.

"You don't trust yourself anymore."

I didn't trust myself. My body randomly had this unprovoked, life-threatening, traumatic brain injury and I had no idea where it came from or how to prevent it from happening again. Being scared was an understatement, I was terrified. How could I not trust myself? How do I even move forward like that? Guilt accompanied that fear because I knew that in admitting I didn't trust myself, I also implied that I didn't trust the Divine dwelling inside me. But God knows what lies within our hearts. He knows all our fears, emotions, even the deepest, darkest secrets we don't dare to tell a soul. Though I didn't want to give life to this thought lurking in my mind, I felt so much freer without it living inside my head.

With that fear off my chest, I admitted how terrified I was to clean my house. I was aware the cleaning products didn't cause the aneurysm, but I had this semi-irrational fear that just a whiff of Clorox bleach or citrus Fabuloso would send me back to the hospital. I vented about how difficult it was carrying around such heaviness, while feeling forced to only portray a partial of the extremes I was feeling. I was so grateful to be alive, and empowered to walk in this second chance God granted me. That was genuine. But I was also extremely sad about what I had to say goodbye to in accepting that second chance. I was extremely overwhelmed with how abruptly my life was turned upside down with only a whopping two months to steady myself, dust off the evidence and keep it moving.

I couldn't do it. I texted my manager to let her know I preferred to have the rest of the week and I could return virtually next week to give myself more time.

Gwen talked with me until I'd fully calmed down, with only the stutter breaths left after such an intense let-out. I shed a few tears of joy or heartbreak since the incident, but I always quickly recovered and kept it moving. This morning was the first time since the moment I experienced a life-changing brain bleed that I allowed myself to cry. The Bible doesn't tell us not to feel our emotions, and God never told us that we could not cry. Ecclesiastes 3:1-8 makes space for the duality of the human experience, stating there's "a time to weep and a time to laugh, a time to mourn and a time to dance."

In my belief that God saved my life, I felt I was obligated to focus only on the celebration and not the suffering that accompanied it. Make no mistake, as believers, it is encouraged that we find contentment in all our situations as written in Philippians 4:12. But because we serve a perfect God, His expectation was never that we be perfect, too. So, it is okay to experience both celebration and suffering, or even suffering amid celebration. It was okay to be grateful that God spared my life while also sad that I had a quarter of hair missing, with a tacky broken heart to match. It was okay to walk in my miraculous physical healing while giving my emotions and my mental health a little more time to catch up.

That realization made me feel a lot better. I was the only one putting these unrealistic expectations on myself. I was a miracle, but what made it miraculous is that it wasn't in *my* strength, and it would never be. I took the rest of the week off. I worked from home that next Monday, and I banked my physical return to the office on Tuesday with 40% being in a good place mentally and 60% on a successful roller set in the morning.

* * *

I fluffed out my curls, grabbed my things for the day and headed to Techwood Drive for my official return to work. My direct supervisor had stayed in touch while I was out of work. She helped with all the HR things, sent a virtual card signed by the team, and even arranged for a virtual Postmates gift card while I was in the hospital. Besides my coworker-turned-homegirl, Maia, and one of the only other few black teammates whom I started the job with and was partnered with, I didn't personally hear from anyone else. It was a sting but honestly not much of a surprise. I tried to suppress these feelings before heading in for the first in-person all staff meeting.

I walked in late and settled into a seat in the back while our vice president was wrapping his intro and segueing to the next speaker. She was the head of a different creative department. She started her presentation by making space for a member of her team who was currently out of work due to a severe medical reason. She emphasized how important it was that she was showered in support and love. Her address and contact information were provided, with her consent, to send gifts and goodies There was an oversized physical card waiting in the back for us to sign. I can't remember if she covered anything else, but I was so put off by what happened that my mind blanked the rest of the meeting.

I obviously can't say what was the level of concern shown while I was away. I wasn't there. But I know that Maia would have mentioned it if any grand gestures were made in my absence, since she'd kept me in the loop. This was not mentioned because it was not done. She mentioned that our manager gave the team my cell, so it stung even more that no one reached out to me, not even the people I'd been working with directly and heavily supporting the past couple of weeks. I was only junior staff, but it still cut deep that no grand gesture was made for me. It reaffirmed my dissatisfaction with my job, knowing I needed a workplace where I was valued as more than just an employee. I had to work hard not to resent my co-workers, but it was difficult to work with people every day, most of whom didn't even bother to ask why I'd been gone for so long. This coupled with my newfound realization that I wasn't quite ready to return in the first place started to fester.

I was back on a job where it seemed nobody cared about me. I got physically exhausted a lot sooner. I was hundreds of miles away from my support system again. I was devoting more time to God, but I felt like I was beginning to struggle more than I had when the incident first happened. I was so confused at the onset of all these sudden overwhelming feelings. The spiritual warfare that ensued came on just like the aneurysm: suddenly and with so much force all I could do was cry out to God to make sense of what was happening.

For weeks, I struggled with everything because of the loud voices in my ear lying to me. I was unable to show up for myself which led to being unable to show up for others. I fell through on obligations and flaked on things I initially felt empowered to do without regard to the consequences because I was in so much mental anguish. In turn, I lost friendships, which only caused me to spiral more. I felt so out of control of everything.

How dare you walk out of my life when I just almost lost it?

It was especially difficult because not many knew about the demons I was battling. I still struggled with portraying only the blessings and miracles.

I desperately needed answers, but nothing made sense. I prayed for help, but it seemed as if my Heavenly Father, who never left my side in that hospital, was nowhere to be found now. Therapy didn't help. I felt like I was incessantly crying and calling my friends. I felt bad for even calling because the conversations were always focused on my sadness, so I stopped. Negativity won. The dark, heavy emotions officially overtook me.

I don't even understand why I'm feeling this way. I can't even explain what I'm feeling. I'm not supposed to be here. I don't understand why God saved me. Who am I? What am I here for?

These internal feelings started to manifest externally as social anxiety, a fear of everything, a lack of boundaries and trust in myself, and the inability to think or converse properly without being in my head. My confidence was at zero. I couldn't even say no to things or people I knew I wasn't in the space for, because I couldn't and wasn't truly showing up as me. Relationships that I cherished were damaged. I desperately needed people to see me—to save me—but I couldn't translate that. I was spiraling out of control, and I couldn't understand how I was just on top of the world, overjoyed to be alive and empowered to truly live in this second chance. Now, here I was wishing that I'd just died in that hospital instead.

I couldn't tell you which terrified me more, the voices in my head convincing me that I shouldn't be alive or the ghastly reflection in the mirror. For weeks, I watched myself morph into this unrecognizable version of me that was seized by fear and ensnared by death: I was a living personification of Psalm 116:3. I was unaware that it's not that I was fighting my battle alone, but that I had no weapons to fight the warfare. I was dragging this hollow version of myself around Atlanta in pursuit of filling the emptiness and feeling something, anything, other than confusion and pain.

But God is so intentional, that one of these seemingly uneventful outings led me to my answers and my breakthrough.

I was invited to a Harvard alumni event with a new divine connection, Mia, whom I was introduced to by a mutual friend. We surrounded a high-top cocktail table with other Harvard alumni, white half-finished small plates lined the black tablecloth. We were casually chatting about church. I asked for recommendations since I was unsuccessfully church hopping in pursuit of a new house of worship. Mia perked up, excitedly inviting me to Change Night in Atlanta, an evening pop-up worship experience hosted by the church she frequented in Jersey. I accepted the invite, eager to fill my days with something meaningful and expand our connection.

A couple of weeks later, I fought the Sunday six p.m. traffic and braved the drive to Austell, Georgia. As I pulled into the Riverside Epicenter, I was overwhelmed with the number of cars in the parking lot. Still COVID cautious, I tossed on my mask and made my way in, texting Mia to see if I could locate her in the mass of people already seated in the dimly lit auditorium.

I spotted the section where Mia and a friend saved me a seat. I was a few minutes late so the praise and worship team were already onstage. The atmosphere was already saturated. I got settled and began detachedly singing along to the songs. The energy was already charged with the presence of God, but I didn't intentionally come for that. But God is such an intentional orchestrator.

As Dr. Daniels walked out and started to pray over the fading praise and worship, the environment shifted from energetic to invocational. Like most services, this is when you're invited to make your worship personal, calling on God specifically for what you need while His presence settles into the room. In my prayer, I asked for healing, peace, answers, and the ability to keep moving forward, because I felt very stuck. We sealed our supplications with an "amen" and took our seats as he transitioned into his message.

The projection screen transitioned to the title of his message as he teased the audience on the topic for the evening.

It read, "I Don't Need Closure." *Okay. I'm paying attention.*

He immediately began to minister to my spirit and my situation, coming in hot with a heavy revelation for the soft break-up I'd just experienced with a word from the book of Samuel.

Okay, God. I heard you. I receive it.

As the message progressed, I sat up so far to the edge of my seat that a housefly landing on my shoulder could've knocked me out of the chair. I was locked in because there wasn't a shadow of a doubt that this message was exactly for me. The literal answers to my prayers couldn't have come any clearer. I was amazed. God ensured I was introduced to Mia at perfect timing to be invited to her alma mater's alumni event. One that I was in no way an alumnus of. And He made sure that we had a conversation about church so that I could find my way to this pop-up service in Austell, an hour's journey with dreadful Atlanta traffic. He is so very intentional.

From understanding that God orchestrates endings and entrances, to plateauing in our progress due to the inability to move on without an explanation, it became more personal.

"I've got to be willing to move on in seasons where there is no explanation," he preached.

The room was silent.

"...Are y'all okay?"

No. I was in tears at this point. I felt so seen, an emotion I lacked the past couple of weeks. If you're not familiar with the book of Job, it is the book in the Bible that tells of a well-off man named Job. God gave Satan permission to test him because of his loyalty and devotion to God. Job lost his livestock, his home, his family and eventually his health. Although Job was ill-advised by friends and his wife, and even began to personally lament for chapters on end, he held on, and God eventually restored his health and wealth with twice as much as he had before. With the interpretation at hand, the focus was on Job's inability to understand why he was suffering in the first place, but instead to understand and accept there simply would not be an explanation in God's generous restoration of his life.

Oh. My. Gosh... I'm Job.

Well, not technically. Obviously, there are some dissimilarities between Job and me. But this experience, this trial, this inexplicable warfare was all in the book of Job. And just like Job, I lamented, questioned, and even went so far as curse my own life because I was so wrapped in the reasons and explanations, that I was neglecting the revelation. For the past few weeks, I was focused on believing that God wasn't speaking. I just didn't give Him time to speak because, like Job, I was too busy filling the space with everything except Him—everything except the Word; His words; His truths.

But here I was in my own chapter 38, with God finally speaking. After verses, pages and chapters of lamenting and mourning, God was here in this room reminding me, just like He did with Job, that HE was sovereign, not us.

"God never told Job why," Dr. Daniels said as he began to end his message over soft, *closing chords.*

"So he's got to move into this next season of his life without an explanation as to why he went through what he went through in the last... And that's who I came for tonight. That's who God put this word on my heart for."

Basing his next teaching on the scripture, Philippians 4:19–*"But my God shall supply all your needs according to his riches in glory by Christ Jesus"* (KJV)–he spoke the final word that sealed the peace I desperately needed to move forward.

"So [Holy Spirit said] 'Dharius, do you believe I supply all your needs?' Yes. 'Okay, so if you needed an explanation in order to have closure I would have gave you one'... I came today to talk to some people who were hearing this word. And I want to announce to you it's time to move on. It's time to go forward. It's time to step into your future. The glory of the latter house is greater than the glory of the former. Remember not the former things, neither consider the things of old, behold I'll do a new thing shall you not know it..."

I was one of those people. I didn't need closure. I didn't need answers. I didn't need a reason. I didn't need an explanation. I just needed to know God was still here with me. As tears streamed down my face, eyes closed focusing on the spiritual and not the emotional, I told God I just needed to know He didn't bring me this far just to bring me this far. To move forward, I accepted that I wouldn't lean into all that I don't know, but instead, lean into what I do know: God is in control. God is a healer. God is a miracle-worker. God is still here: He never left.

In case there was any room for the analytic in me to start to question whether this was all merely a coincidence, he said:

"I want you to receive this word as God's love letter for you. I want you to receive this word as a way of God saying to you, 'I love you so much. I gave him this for you, and I gave him this word on this day for you, because this is your season to move. You need to move now. I gave it to you now because it's not too late. The devil's telling you it's too late, it's not too late...The devil is a LIAR...'"

That phrase—which can easily fall into a rhythm of being just any old Christian rhetoric—was reinforced as my weapon.

He released a healing prayer for the broken-hearted, and I released the weeks of pain, confusion and suffering. I cried my last tear, knowing it wouldn't be my last tear ever, but my last tear of defeat. I released the heaviness I came in with and received my answers, healing, and breakthrough.

I left the hospital back in April feeling free from the physical chains that seemingly had me bound: The bedrest, the IVs and EKGs, the IVD tube, the chair alarms—and I thought my fight was over. When the physical didn't work, the enemy tried to attack me mentally. After failing to kill me with a rupture and bleeding on the brain, he tried to make me think I was losing my mind and that I should've died in that hospital. And for a second, he was winning. But that day in June, I left the Riverside Epicenter feeling free from the last bit of chains the enemy attempted to wrap around my mind.

Without those chains yoking me to the devil and his herd of demons, I was free to graze in much greener pastures that my Shepherd was finally able to lead me into.

10

Recovery. Revival. Rebirth.

"And I knew that the moment I opened my eyes and my hands instantly went into the air, baptized in anesthesia and the blood of Jesus, I resurfaced reborn, and it was my job to be a walking, living, breathing testimony to whatever this grand plan is God has for me..."

I tore through my closet like a madwoman on Sunday morning to find something to wear. Service started at 10 a.m. I had almost two hours to get ready, but I knew how easy it was for time to pass by as I slipped in and out of various clothing combinations. It had been two years since I attended church in person and all my clothes were either too casual or too small. I eventually settled on some burnt orange flowy pants, a cream button-down, and a pair of nude pumps. I clasped the latch on my gold braided, herringbone necklace before stepping back to give the combo a final look in the mirror.

Okay, we like this!

I grabbed my final accessory, a black surgical mask, and went out the door after making a quick Sunday fit-check TikTok. I was excited to return to a physical house of worship, but I knew the excitement was mostly in finding *my* new house of worship. After being ministered to and unintentionally finding peace in the word of God after weeks of confusion and darkness, I knew this would be the first step to walking into greener pastures God was leading me into. I also started reading the Bible cover to cover and increasing my devotional time. This was an action on the promise I made in the hospital to truly get to know Christ; a part of my conscious decision to give God my intentional yes.

During my devotional, I was excited to turn the page of the stories we're all familiar with at night. As I read, bouncing around the books following a suggested order from Facebook that I saved but failed to start at the beginning of the year, I felt I was getting a realistic and digestible picture of Jesus the man, not just God the Almighty. It was like the secrets of the universe were being unlocked before me, every night that I tapped the burgundy Holy Bible icon and tapped into the history of Christianity and its Father.

I continued receiving so much revelation from every service in my journey to find a church home. The first was a prophecy at my home church after sharing my testimony for the first time. I was told God was "preserving me" to lead my generation. The next was a word from an apostle on a community Zoom prayer call. We never met before and I couldn't even tell you the man's name today, but amidst prayer, he called my name out of a catalog of inactive cameras. He told me that although I'm going through a season right now that I didn't understand, God said that what the enemy meant for evil, He is using it to build me. I was again strengthened by Reverend Warnock and his interpretation of Jacob wrestling with the angel of God in Genesis at a jazz Sunday service in the park. I left with the revelation of blessings in broken places, and an understanding of being "bruised and blessed, broken and blossoming."

I was amazed to see how beautifully the word of God caressed my scars. I'd gone through weeks and weeks of mental torment. I was inconsolable

RECOVERY. REVIVAL. REBIRTH.

and unable to find peace in or with anything of this world. But receiving prophetic messages I later learned were all steeped in scripture gave me the comfort I'd been scrambling for. The peace that surpassed understanding was found every time I stumbled upon or received scripture that spoke directly to my situation and told me exactly how to move forward.

As I sought God first, I realized everything else was falling into place. My peace returned to me. Whenever my world attempted to be shaken, I knew how to return to solid ground. My confidence came back, and I was empowered to pursue opportunities in freelance writing and hosting, a dream of mine that I'd felt I was too stuck to pursue pre-aneurysm. I released the anger I'd been harboring at work and began to take initiative. This led to me being able to take on more projects. I picked up performing again, returning to my favorite weekly open night experience, then called *Poetry on Peters,* where my return was embraced with open arms after sharing 'Testimony II' live for the first time. After a chat with my therapist, I was encouraged to start my podcast, "The Heat Sheet." Reflecting on that initial conversation that made me 'just do it,' I realized the revelation in one of her insightful sentiments.

"Nothing would ever get done if everybody waited until they had everything together. Just start it, and figure it out along the way," she said.

So, I did. And my personal stories podcast–initially recorded on a $7 Amazon lavalier microphone from my college journalism days–later transitioned into a full-blown Christian podcast for season two, based entirely on the Word. I picked up one of my journals one day, flipping through the pages to scribble in some notes from a sermon, and I realized there was a checklist from my very rough first few months in Atlanta back in 2021. It was titled *"Things to make ATL feel like home."* Listed under it were unchecked items that I'd been able to accomplish in the last month alone by simply seeking a closer relationship with God.

My life was becoming a living version of Matthew 6:33. By chasing God first, all the things I said I needed were seemingly handed to me. I was walking with purpose and power. I felt so driven to do things that scared me, and to pursue things that poured into me. I was learning the Word, growing my relationship with God, sharing my story everywhere I went, while training my ear and heart to be sensitive to His voice and direction.

My intentional walk led me right to my new house of worship, the dReam Center Church of Atlanta. A year later, I received the divine assignment to write this book. I usually attend the 10 a.m. service but struggled to wake up early that Sunday and opted for the noon service instead. As I settled into the pew, still about 10 minutes late but right on time, I received confirmation of the random thought of writing a book that dropped in my spirit on the drive over. As I was putting my things down and focusing on the words of the prayer, I felt called to attention by the divine directive to *"get out the book, take your pen and write down your story...because God is going to save lives through it."*

After attending the service for the first time in my church search, the power of God was so heavy in the room that I was moved to return for another service the next Sunday instead of visiting the next church on my list. During my first visit, I stumbled in just in time for the release of Bishop William Murphy's newest album, *Worship and Justice.* He would celebrate the release the following Sunday by performing some of the songs live. Of course, I had to return for the concert.

I was in a much better space, but I still subconsciously battled the thoughts of complications with the aneurysm in the first couple of months. Any remaining questions of whether I was in the right place melted away after having my long-time favorite gospel artist-turned-Bishop minister *"The Just Shall Live"* live in a house saturated with the presence of God. I stood at the altar alongside others wrestling with physical illness or infirmities, eyes closed, and hands lifted. Once again, the declaration floated around me like a warm dessert scent trail, *"You shall live and not die."*

I showed up each Sunday, excited to be in the house until I eventually got looped into serving on leadership. Each Sunday I gave God a yes, he'd show up in a different area of my life and give me one. I was finally in a season where things made sense again. I might not have received a 'why' in the last season, but I was receiving a 'what' for the next one. I acknowledge that God's plan for us is more complex and grander than anything we could comprehend. But all the things I questioned in the last season felt much clearer in this one.

I didn't receive an explanation for those things, yet there was a new level of clarity moving forward. I still wrestle with my Atlanta residency occasionally. But I can't imagine having been in Ahoskie during my medical emergency, where the nearest center with a neuro team would've been a helicopter transport away. I was battling bouts of imposter syndrome and post-grad depression. It kept me paralyzed and perched firmly on top of stories, ideas and gifts that I refused to die sitting on after this experience, after being so close to death. *"Find a church home"* would still be a scribble in a journal without the fire to truly get to know the God who saved my life. Now I'm on fire for Him, using those gifts as an ambassador for the Kingdom, learning and growing each day.

And that has made all the difference.

Life has continued to go on. It's still full of trials and trauma, tests and turbulence but the difference now is that I am truly rooted.

There's still loss, but I understand how to maneuver through my season of mourning and keep moving. There are still troubles, but I know that they don't last always. There's still pain, but I am a first-hand witness that there's a God near to the brokenhearted and those crushed in spirit. There's still warfare like never before, but now I have a weapon to fight back.

Everything that I needed was birthed in the trial of this moment: community, motivation, purpose, freedom. Before, I naively believed that I'd been doing life all on my own. Losing my brother in 2020 was the first hard reality check that I was not and would never be in control. That terrified me. But even when I felt too broken and betrayed to pray, I still felt drawn to God. The aneurysm would once again remind me of just that: That I am not in control, but in a gentler, comforting way when my mortality was at play.

Now I'm keenly aware of the presence of God in my life like never before, a realization I firmly believe I may have never stepped into so soon had it not been for my experience. That awareness comes with so much power. A certain persuasion comes with knowing your Father—once you accept and are obedient to Him—will move Heaven and earth for you if you ask and believe.

I stayed generally encouraged in the hospital because of the obvious disbelief of my reports and my village of prayer warriors. There's something affirming about seeing the faces of nonbelievers and skeptics. Doctors who trusted medicine over the Most High. Nurses who couldn't understand how I managed to be so confident. Techs who could believe how fast I was recovering. As alarming as it should've been that the natural doctors couldn't explain why it happened, where it came from, or how in the world I was up and at the capacity that I was following, it gave me peace. This was no ordinary experience. It was far from it. It was a supernatural experience that would completely change my life forever. I'd always been a believer. I'd always been a lover of Christ. But I could never deny or fail to prioritize him ever again after personally holding his hand and having the Holy Spirit carry me through that hospital.

I was so grounded in faith that I was so far removed by what happened or could've happened to me, that sometimes I didn't quite understand people's reactions.

Like seeing one of my best friends, a newly graduated nurse. She understood all too well the severity of my condition, so she burst into tears after seeing me for the first time in the middle of her graduation party.

Or the prolonged hugs from friends who usually respected my awkward relationship, or lack thereof, to extended physical touch.

Or shocked looks from passersby asking my mom how I was doing, just for her to casually deflect to say, "she's right here."

Or the invitations to be with family who "just wanted to lay eyes on me for themselves."

Or lunch with a loved one who asked me, "Jazmine do you even know the odds?"

It dawned on me.

I was not supposed to be here.

I didn't subscribe to that mindset because I didn't walk in that belief. I didn't know whether it was sheer delusion or what I believed to be an instinctual flex of my faith muscle. I just fully walked in this healing and recovery God laid out for me. I was walking by faith in the best way possible.

So that's a lie, from the father of lies himself. I am supposed to be here, because God is intentional. I'm supposed to be the shock factor that makes you jump back and grab your chest in disbelief in the middle of a dollar store. My healing, recovery, and story are part of God's plan to remind His people that He is still the God of Lazarus and the God of Moses. He's still the God that told the man to take up his bed and walk, or that confirmed to the woman that her faith had healed her. My testimony shows that we still serve a God in the business of miracles, signs and wonders.

"It's either hereditary or bad luck."

It didn't make sense initially because that was a part of the testimony. I can no longer accept that my aneurysm was a freak accident or random occurrence. And I'm not unlucky. I'm the furthest thing from it. Bishop Murphy taught us that something is from God when it feels bigger than you. Beyond what your strength or skills could accomplish, and your intellect can comprehend. I unintentionally understood the assignment when those words from the doctor activated the Divine Presence that dwelled in me. Still, I couldn't wrap my mind around it at first because it was a part of God's plan that none of us could ever perceive.

I didn't just turn to him out of obligation. It's not simply *'he saved my life, so I now owe it to him'* though that is correct. But because God—such a merciful and generous father—blessed me, saved me and was faithful to me even when I wasn't even faithful to Him? I decided I've got to know how good it can get if I give him everything. So, I did. I have. Every day I wake up and choose him. Every single day I wake up and give him a conscious yes.

Like many of us, I felt like I had all the time in the world. I never considered how death could knock on my door at a moment's notice, ready to hand me my eviction. I was reminded of the fragility of life, and how very delicate it is to be alive. My experience awakened me with a jolt, showing me how close we must sometimes get to death to truly understand the value of life. God decided to preserve my life and my mind. Waking up after a procedure overflowing with risks, the decision was all mine: To wade back to my old life and who I was before, or to walk in my newness across the glistening waters to one chock-full of second chances.

I chose the latter, riding the wave of freedom that comes with releasing the weights that threaten to take you under. Christians are baptized in water to symbolize Christ's death, burial, and resurrection. Under the water, lies the acceptance that we will be washed clean of our sins. You accept that you must say goodbye to who you were before going under because you will be new once you come up.

In the heat of the moment, I refused to say goodbyes beforehand, but I remember a farewell sitting on my spirit that I couldn't quite figure out. It wasn't to my loved ones, because I had the assurance God would bring me out to see them again. But the revelation now is I was saying goodbye to me; the old me that'd be put under and buried, intending to rise again a new person, resurrected after my anesthesia baptism.

Epilogue

Six months later, my close friend, Alex and I sat in front of my laptop reading the pre- and post-procedure instructions, while the bright orange and red Piedmont logo beamed back at us.

"Please be sure to arrive at 6:00 A.M."

Funny enough, with all the bolded red text and highlighted medical warnings, *that* was the scariest thing listed on the page.

I was returning to Piedmont Atlanta for my first six-month postoperative follow up. They would perform a diagnostic angiogram to get a detailed x-ray of the blood vessels in my brain. This, as opposed to the simpler MRI scans, would be more invasive and require anesthesia again. The procedure uses a long, flexible catheter that is entered into the artery by either femoral access via my groin or radial access in my wrist. I was given discharge instructions on both, with the femoral access looking to be the more restrictive procedure.

Let's hope they'll go for radial access.

Either way, I knew I wouldn't be driving home following the procedure and be restricted to taking it easy for the rest of the day. I didn't have Nurse Mom here to take care of me this time as planned due to a broken leg, but I was blessed with a best friend kind enough to fly in from Memphis, Tennessee to help me after my procedure. After talking her through the maze of a hospital that is Piedmont Atlanta, I set out my clothes and prayed for a safe procedure, calling it an early night in preparation for our early morning.

Naturally, I was nervous about going back under anesthesia. Adrenaline, pain and faith overrode any ounce of fear during my emergency procedure, and anything was better than the splitting head pain and discomfort I was feeling then. But general medical jitters aside, I wasn't worried. I was empowered. I'd been studying the Word, attending church and walking boldly while growing my relationship with Christ. If I trusted him then with the mustard seed-sized faith and relationship I had, I can only imagine the miracle I was about to walk into with my bigger faith and relationship. I told everyone I was in faith for good news and a miraculous recovery, even down to enacting how I imagined the doctor's responses would be when I woke up.

Miss Bunch, we can't believe it. We don't know how, but there's not even a trace of aneurysm!

To which I'd casually reply, *"I can, God did it!"*

A generic Amazon alarm tone blasted through my Alexa at 5:30 A.M., gently pulling me out of a light sleep cycle. Since my clothes were already out, all I had to do was wake up, freshen up and be on our way. I drove to the hospital, gospel music playing softly through the radio as we rode to the hospital. Traffic was light so it was an easy drive to Piedmont Atlanta. Upon pulling up and parking, I couldn't tell whether the feeling in my stomach was nerves, uneasiness from being up so early, or protest from my midnight fast. Before turning off the car, I grabbed Alex's hand and we prayed.

This time felt different than my initial stint in the hospital. My prayers in the emergency room came from a place of desperation then. That morning, my prayers came from a place of declaration and expectation. I'd been in faith for a total recovery, so I believed it was so. I'd been walking boldly in my healing, so I had full expectation that I could believe my way into it: today would only provide physical confirmation.

We weaved through the network of long hallways to each check-in point and waiting room. After receiving a COVID test and a series of labs, we were escorted to the final waiting area for procedure patients. I was soon greeted by a friendly assistant in scrubs who escorted us into the procedure area. It was always interesting when the medical staff asked what brings me in for all the brain-related imaging I'd receive that day. I assumed they'd have my entire file, but I guess I assumed incorrectly as they were always so taken aback when I told them I was a year removed from surviving a brain aneurysm.

Wow, and you're only 24 years old?
  Oh my, but you're so young.
  Well, you have made quite the recovery.

We continued to chat as we made our way toward the curtained room where I'd be occupying a bed. I was instructed to change into the hospital gown and remove all jewelry. Stepping back into the hospital gown after six months felt daunting. It was such a heavy symbol of my time in the hospital. As long as I wore that gown, I felt like I was wearing my infirmity. Dressed in blue, I was a patient. People are only patients when something is wrong. But I pushed back the thought and reminded myself that I was only a patient for a day, and after my procedure I'd be shedding that gown and walking out of Piedmont Atlanta with good news once again.

A very friendly black nurse came in to check all my vitals and give me another rundown of the procedure, while exchanging pleasantries with Alex and me. As she prepped the blood pressure machine, I was once again taken through the lengthy list of risks associated with the procedure:

Blood clotting, allergic reaction, blindness, stroke, heart attack, seizures, infection, complications with the anesthesia or paralysis among others.

The risks rang in my head a lot louder than they did in the emergency room in April. The only thing that snapped me out of this trance was her asking if

I had already set up my advanced directive.

"I'm sorry, a what?" I asked. "What do I need that for?"

As she began to cuff my arm to collect my blood pressure, she explained that creating my advanced directive lets the doctors know what to do if I were to become seriously ill, or if I couldn't communicate my wishes.

As if I wasn't already struggling to maintain my courage after playing minesweeper with the list of risks, this final question sent me over the edge.

Was I going to die today? Does she know something that I don't know about this procedure? Why on earth would she ask me that? And why would she ask me that directly after giving me a fun list of ways to do so, and directly before putting me under anesthesia for a procedure?

While the nurse was facing the monitor and conversing with Alex, I attempted to calm myself down. I forgot she'd already slid the blood pressure sleeve on my arm. Looking back, it's almost comical how the two were chattering in concern over my dramatically high numbers while I was attempting to stop the oncoming nervous attack.

"It looks like your blood pressure is really high, I wonder what is wrong with this machine–" she said, before glancing at me.

My face was red, eyes lined with tears, and very embarrassed.

"Oh no, don't cry, it's going to be okay," she said.

She assured me everything she'd gone over was standard practice. They always ask patients about advanced directives. But something about it coupled with the myriad of risks and a recent brain aneurysm didn't sit too well with me. I let the rest of the tears flow, we breathed through that moment, and my blood pressure returned to a level suitable to move forward with the procedure. After seeing the physical result of getting so worked up, I remembered how confidently I walked into the hospital this morning and wondered where that went.

Come on, Jazmine. The same God that kept you then, will keep you again. If fear is in the room, where is faith going to go?

And after regulating my mind, body and spirit, I was back at ease, with a textbook reminder of what fear and worry can do. We'd called my mom before I was rolled away from Alex and back into the procedure room. Like the first time but much less frantically, I was transferred to a small flat table and prepped for the procedure. I was attached to cords, monitors and the works while the anesthesiologist gave me the heads up that they were going to start the IV anesthetic as she placed the oxygen mask over my mouth and nose.

"Deep breaths, in and out," were the last words she coached as I drifted off.

* * *

I woke up disoriented and with a sore throat from the endotracheal tube. The nurses moving about directed their attention to me once they noticed I was awake. I was starting to get oriented when out of the corner popped Dr. S's neurosurgery assistant, J.

"Hi Miss Jazmine," she cooed, "Safe procedure, everything went well but they did find something. You're still coming off the anesthesia so Dr. S and I will follow up with more information,"

They found something? Cue the tinnitus-heartbeat-head spinning feeling.

That didn't sound at all like *"miraculous recovery"* or *"the aneurysm is gone."* That didn't sound at all like the miracle I was expecting.

My throat was sore, and she walked away too quickly for me to respond. I also didn't have the words. I laid there crushed and confused wondering what went wrong. They rolled me back into the room to a smiling Alex, who I assumed they'd already given an update. They reviewed my discharge instructions, walking me through the specifics of a femoral access discharge. My wrist proved to be uncooperative, so they had to enter through my groin. We scheduled my telehealth visit to discuss the results with the neurosurgeon. Alex helped me get dressed before parting ways to pull the car around to meet the nurse who'd wheel me to the pickup point.

I got into the car carefully and buckled my seatbelt. We took a right onto the same Peachtree Road I'd just rode down feeling victorious. Only this time, the ride was solemn and silent. We made a pit stop at the Chick-fil-A to grab breakfast, but I didn't have an appetite despite not eating in over 12 hours. I was so discouraged and dare I say, disappointed? God saved my life and performed miracle after miracle while I was in the ICU. I'd been intentional the past few months about truly seeking a relationship and having faith. I'd even successfully completed my first corporate fast with my new church, where I met God with the expectation that my sacrifice was in faith for a total recovery. Why wasn't I healed?

What did they see? Did I not fast correctly? What did I do wrong?

I wasn't in the mood to talk, so I quickly texted my loved ones waiting for an update to let them know the procedure went well and that I'd be resting for the next few hours. I laid on my couch with Alex nearby and Netflix on. I cycled through all the thoughts and questions running rampant in my head until I finally drifted off into a nap.

I woke up feeling rested but still far from at ease. *What did they see?* To pile on the drama, not long after waking from my nap, I received a call from the surgeon's assistant J, swapping my telephone visit for an in-office consultation with her and Dr. S to discuss next steps and *"treatment."*

Treatment?! What did they see?

Now, I was mortified. After being assured that we'd discuss my results at the visit, we ended the call with me accepting an entire week of anxiety, worrying and wondering about what could be wrong. Throughout the rest of the day, I finally returned the concerned calls of loved ones letting them know I didn't get the news we'd hoped for. I was poured into with prayer and encouragement, but I just couldn't shake the feeling of discouragement that sat on me.

I was crushed. I couldn't understand what I did wrong. What happened? These last six months have been the closest to God I've ever been, and I wasn't healed. Yet, when my life was saved in April, I was the furthest thing from a saved lifestyle. My disappointment indicated that I'd truly walked in faith all this time. I thought I could receive a clean bill of health if I just believed in it. If that was the case, why didn't that happen?

Anesthesia and the long morning exhausted me for the rest of the day, so we lounged out watching Netflix. I put the anxious thoughts in the back of my mind and allowed the problems of the fictional, Netflix-original characters to fall front and center. After hours of indulging in the imagined realities, it was time to return to my reality and go to bed. I would've normally washed some of the heaviness away with a hot shower, but I was on strict orders to avoid showering the first night while the puncture site on my groin healed. I retreated to my room where I cried alone but remembered I had one of my favorite minds and fervent believers on the other side of the wall. I was so used to being alone and going through things by myself in Atlanta that I almost missed the blessing God conveniently flew into Atlanta, just for me. I shuffled back into the living room, red and wet in the face.

"I was going to cry alone in my room, but I decided not to," I said before bursting into tears, "Alex, I'm so scared."

We never discussed what the doctors said since I assumed they'd given her a report. But that didn't matter as her faith instantly kicked in, supplementing where mine was lacking. We talked through David and Psalms, a book in the Bible full of natural, human emotions that David was experiencing. Alongside that lovely advice, she assured me of unlocking new levels of faith that'd been pushed to me all day, but I was so deep in lamenting that I refused to receive it.

For the third time that day, I was reminded it wasn't over. My mom comforted me earlier that day with the thought that maybe it still could be nothing, to which I was annoyed. How could it be nothing if the doctors said they saw something? But then I realized, whose word you believe, God or the doctors? This wasn't the end. Whether it was something or not, their diagnosis was not the end-all, be-all. They don't have the final say-so, God does.

My first mistake was believing that God's movement is based on what we do right or wrong, or what we can or can't do. Though I walked in faith for my healing, I set myself up for disappointment by thinking His action was based on anything I've done. I saw this the first time He so graciously saved my life in an act of faithfulness when I wasn't even faithful to Him. His goodness isn't and never will be based on my ability, my strength, heck, not even my faith or belief. But it is still my job as a believer to believe until it happens, and to give him the praise when it does. I was simply walking into new levels of faith. So, I walked out of my discouragement and into that next week with the assurance that God is still in control.

* * *

I took the day off work for my appointment to spend the morning at home before heading into the vascular neurosurgery office. I stared at the Halloween decorations the office was adorned in for far too long while I waited in the lobby. When they finally called me to the back, I quickly called my mom on FaceTime so she could also hear the news in real time.

Dr. S and assistant J were both in the room for the appointment. Dr. S exchanged pleasantries with my mom over the phone before discussing whatever I was here in person for. He had his n95 respirator hanging around his neck, and I realized this was the first time I'd seen his entire face. I opted for a sweater dress and light jacket that morning since it was chilly outside, but the windowless room was small and hot. They were seated across the room, where posters of the brain and its anatomy lined the walls. I wonder how many life-altering conversations they had in this stuffy little room. I know some patients left overjoyed, with others leaving the patient wondering what next. I wondered which I'd be today.

As I was told the day of the angiogram, they did find something.

Deep breath.

But what they found was so minimal that there was a lower chance of the aneurysm rebleeding or rupturing again than the first time. He gave me the medical rundown of an aneurysm and how they work, but all I could hear ringing in my ears was *"what we found was so minimal..."*

Thank you, Jesus. Thank you once again for your faithfulness.

I had two options; to continue to monitor the aneurysm with an MRI every six months to follow its progress, or proceed to operate, which he cautioned was more actually risky than monitoring. Once again, he paused and gave me the option to choose.

It was a no-brainer. This moment allowed me to choose who I'd put my trust in moving forward.

"You all have done amazing work, but I serve a Power higher than any doctor here," I said. "Let's wait and monitor."

If God can create the world in 7 days, I'm sure he can clear up an aneurysm in six months.

Dr. S nodded in approval of my decision, notating that as long as he was my physician, my care would always be my choice. I fired off a round of questions, from whether I had any restrictions, if I needed to make any lifestyle changes, to the burning question I wanted to be certain there still wasn't a natural answer to.

"And we're still unaware of where exactly this aneurysm came from?" I asked.

Shaking his head, he began to explain the statistics surrounding them, their likelihood and environmental factors that contribute to it happening to varying demographics. Nothing however, that quite pinpointed why it happened to *me.*

I skipped back to my car, struggling to contain the relief that consumed me. True to the declaration made over my life these past few months, I wasn't going to die. I sat in my car praying and thanking God for his faithfulness again, with bits of 1 Peter 5:8 and Hebrews 11:1 sitting on my spirit.

After six months in my relationship with Christ, this moment was an invitation to step into a new level of faith and believing. Of course, believing God for a miracle is easy when it was already done. Believing in the Supernatural is one thing when you receive confirmation of it in the natural realm. I sat in the ICU reveling in faith because God granted me the grace of healing in real time. But to trust Him and have faith when the things around you aren't directly lining up—To trust God despite what you see and still believe when you don't see it yet? *That* is true faith.

Silly of me to believe that the learning stopped when I left the hospital. That the struggle stopped there. God never said there wouldn't be storms. But He could calm them. Faith isn't just getting on the boat with Jesus. It's getting in, sailing down the seas, seeing the storm ahead and not worrying because you have the Messiah in the boat with you. The winds may be blowing, the waters are raging, and He may be sleeping, but He is in the boat, nonetheless.

I struggled with the latter part of *Anesthesia and the Blood of Jesus*. I wrestled with the idea that the last chapters had to end neatly. But as brought to my attention by Alex in another come-to-Jesus moment, life doesn't have storybook endings. Aside from reliving the scary moments, the most difficult part was writing the testimony while still living in it.

But the miracle is that I am still here, able to live in it and tell my story.

I'm constantly running into people who I share my testimony with. I'm always humbled when they share similar stories of loved ones who unfortunately don't share the same fate. I don't take my experience or my healing for granted.

For months, I couldn't understand or accept that I almost died. I couldn't believe I was so close to a completely different reality. I couldn't wrap my head around the fact that I was a mere risk-factor away from no longer being alive. But now I understand that it had to happen, or I wouldn't be walking in spiritual power and awareness like I am today. Each day is its own journey full of learning, opportunity, and chance—not necessarily to get it right—but to get closer to the mark. My heart is forever indebted to the anesthesia and blood of Jesus that washed over and forever changed me.

Testimony II

Sit back for a bit and honey,
  I'll tell you exactly how it feels to be God's favorite.
  I'll tell you how it feels now that I know for sure
  that He knows my name
  I'll even tell you the prayer
  See they've been asking CiCi for hers but see,
  let me tell you 'bout mine.

I told you before I had a testimony
  and the wildest part was that one was only the beginning.
  See, this
  makes that feel merely like
  the warm up.

Just the interlude to the exhibition,
  this grand showing up,
  showing off,
  showing out
  in my life that God does
  So allow me to reintroduce you
  to one of God's biggest flexes.
  Greatest blessings.
  Here is yet another lesson
  for me to tell you, you and you that
  this is my testimony.

Because it's just something about knowing
  I'm walking in so much grace,
  being physically reminded that I'm moving
  in so much power .

That when emergency strikes
  And there's no urgency by man
  I know God is working.
  In overtime.
  On overdrive.

If you ask me,
  I was never wheeled through
  the hallways of a hospital
  I was carried through this battle
  by God's Grace.

And the mind is a terrible thing to waste
  so the enemy knew
  to try to attack the exact place
  where God has this gift of mine
  here.

But God,
  was everywhere.
  He was with me when
  it felt like my brain was on fire
  I heard Him through Sunday service live streaming
  through the Roku,
  Reverend Raphael Warnock's voice bleeding through the room
  over the ringing in my ears,
  he was saying
  We gon' be alright.

We gon' be alright.

So I knew, we
  was gon' be
  alright.

Even though sound was fading and
  light was blinding
  and brain was on fire
  I knew, Rev' said it but God sent it

we was gon' be alright.

I heard someone say once
  fear and doubt are the opposite
  of faith and God
  and it changed my life

So I had no fear in that hospital room because
  why try to fill the space with doubt when God
  was already settled into the room?

The surgeon looked down at me and told me
  I was in good hands.
  Oh, I already know.
  you better know,
  you carrying precious cargo.

'Cause even through inexplicable pain
  they got jokes,
  they got joy from me,
  they got jubilation
  because I had this crazy faith that told me

the battle was already won

You just got this certain persuasion
when you know your Father's gon' move for you.
You move different when you know you got that favor

I didn't even have time to doubt,
my Father who art in Heaven is my biggest flex.

So as they prepped to put me under
I said listen docs,
don't mean to be rude or nun'
but I need a quick 1 on 1
with the Big Dawg out loud
and part of the prayer was
God,
I don't know what part of the plan this is,
or what chapter this gon' be
but I know
it's gon' be one heck of a story

I never laid in the hospital bed
wondering if I was gonna be okay
I knew.

And I knew that the moment I opened my eyes
and my hands instantly went in the air,
baptized in anesthesia and
the blood of Jesus,
I resurfaced reborn.
And it was my job to be a
walking,
living,

breathing,
testimony
to whatever it is God has planned for me.
This vision.
This purpose.
This power
Is of God. From God. All God.

Recovery,
   they told me the worst is behind you now,
   is it?

Because as I lay me down to sleep,
   I pray the Lord my soul to keep
   these aches and pains too much to bear
   I just wasn't sure if I wanted to stay here
   But God,
   in the form of pastors, prayer warriors and
   a fired up momma
   speeding down 85
   pleading the blood and
   coming in slinging holy oil and hand sanitizer
   kept me, reminded me
   it was my turn to fight now,
   and I was not fighting alone.

So we did,
   we fought.

Because if the devil was gonna wage war
   on me like he was trying to, I knew
   I was gonna need armor like no other
   to make it through to tell this story like no other

I stayed prayed up,
healing angels on the walls,
Bible open to the book of Psalms,
God invited into the room

and ain't it something

about knowing that I am walking in so much grace,
feeling that physical reminder that I am
covered by God himself,
I know it, I held His hand.

I'm so blessed, ain't no way I can go back.
Ain't no way I could ever walk the same.
I'd be crazy to, because
I've been reborn.

www.ingramcontent.com/pod-product-compliance
Lightning Source LLC
Chambersburg PA
CBHW020352130626
46549CB00006B/2273